MW00803445

Discover the Further Secrets of:

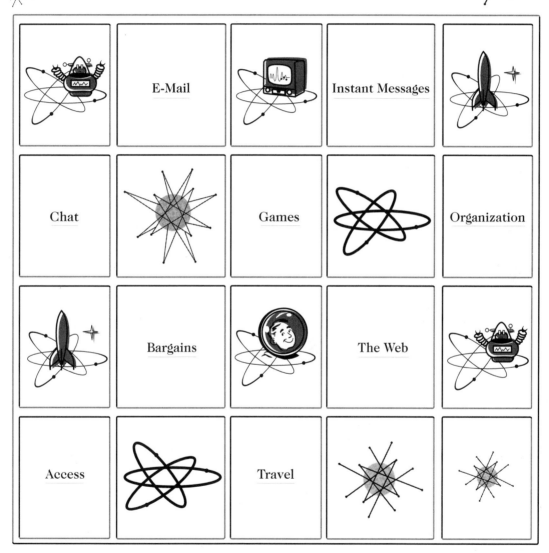

	E-Mail		Instant Messages	
Chat		Games		Organization
	Bargains		The Web	
Access		Travel		

Click your heels together three times to go home...

Updated 1/98

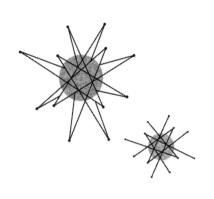

America Online

Amazing Secrets

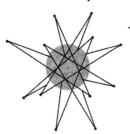

AMERICA ONLINE®

AMAZING SECRETS

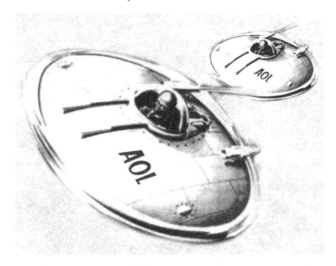

Laura Arendal

SYBEX®   **San Francisco • Paris • Düsseldorf • Soest**

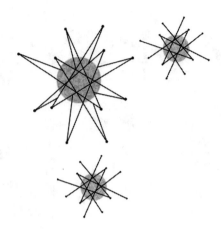

Associate Publisher: Roger Stewart
Contracts and Licensing Manager: Kristine Plachy
Acquisitions & Developmental Editor: Sherry Bonelli
Editor: Alison Moncrieff
Technical Editor: Beth Wiley
Book Designer: Maureen Forys, Chris Gillespie
Electronic Publishing Specialist: Kate Kaminski
Production Coordinator: Grey Magauran
Production Assistants: Beth Moynihan, Rebecca Rider
Indexer: Matthew Spence
Cover Designer: Daniel Zigler
Cover Illustrator: Daniel Zigler
Author Photo: David Dyson

The author and publisher have made their best efforts to prepare this book, and the content is based upon final release software whenever possible. Portions of the manuscript may be based upon pre-release versions supplied by software manufacturer(s). The author and the publisher make no representation or warranties of any kind with regard to the completeness or accuracy of the contents herein and accept no liability of any kind including but not limited to performance, merchantability, fitness for any particular purpose, or any losses or damages of any kind caused or alleged to be caused directly or indirectly from this book.

Photographs and illustrations used in this book have been downloaded from publicly accessible file archives and are used in this book for news reportage purposes only to demonstrate the variety of graphics resources available via electronic access. Text and images available over the Internet may be subject to copyright and other rights owned by third parties. Online availability of text and images does not imply that they may be reused without the permission of rights holders, although the Copyright Act does permit certain unauthorized reuse as fair use under 17 U.S.C. Section 107.

Library of Congress Card Number: 97-81250
ISBN: 0-7821-2229-9

Manufactured in the United States of America

10 9 8 7 6 5 4 3 2 1

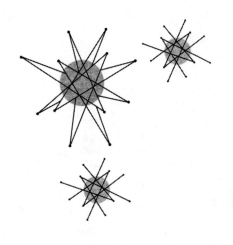

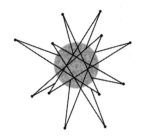

To my grandmother,
Marie B. Mount

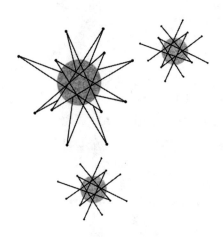

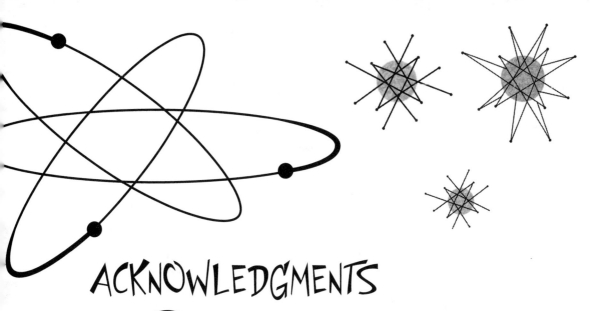

ACKNOWLEDGMENTS

(F)irst and foremost I'd like to thank the unsung heros of the publishing world: the publishing staff. The editors— Acquisitions & Developmental Editor Sherry Bonelli, Editor Alison Moncrieff, and AOL Tech Writer Beth Wiley, who acted as technical editor on this book—were a delight to work with as they gently put me on the right track and kept me there. Once my words had been made acceptable, designers Maureen Forys and Chris Gillespie, Electronic Publishing Specialist Kate Kaminski, and Production Coordinator extraordinaire Grey Magauran made this book glow.

I'd also like to thank my friends, coworkers, and fellow AOLies who helped me throughout this book: Pete Lang, Susan Benston, Paul King, for their chat time; Q13ert and Peter Kuhns for their technical advice; David Krassner for starting me on this whole AOL journey; AOL's Brad Schepp for his help along the way, Carrie Lavine and Dan Brodnitz for giving me my first crack at book revision and getting me involved with books from the writing end; Barbara Gordon for all those vacation days that allowed me to concentrate on my writing; Joe Sikoryak, Steve Gilmartin, Emily Acker, and Paulette Washington for all their support (and Paulette again for all the Pepsi!); Twila, Kaerste, and O'Malley for reminding me of mealtimes and keeping my lap warm; and Dave Dyson for his boolean expertise and for giving me an excuse to shut down my computer when I needed a break.

CONTENTS AT A GLANCE

TABLE OF CONTENTS

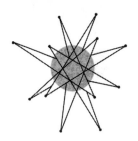

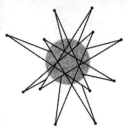

Table of Contents

3 Wowing the Chat Room   71

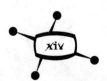

Table of Contents

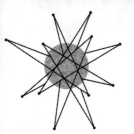

Table of Contents

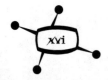

xvi

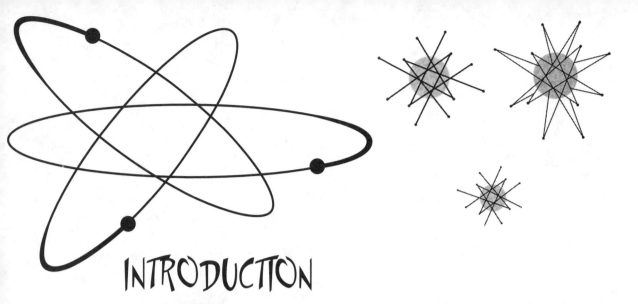

INTRODUCTION

ave you used AOL for a while (or even just signed up for the service), found it pretty easy to move around in, but want to know how you can use the service to your full advantage? You've come to the right place.

This book will zip through the how-tos of AOL's nifty features and concentrate on the obscure details you'll need to know to make your AOL experience the most it can be. From meeting and greeting to finding cool shlag online, this book shows you how to get the very most out of your AOL experience.

WHAT YOU NEED TO USE THIS BOOK

This book was written using AOL 4 on Windows 95. I've included some tips for AOL 3 users, but the pathways indicated and super-duper features explained are straight from AOL 4.

If you're resisting upgrading, let me just say—upgrade! Not only does AOL 4 have some cool new features, such as allowing you to switch screen names without signing off, but it closes the loopholes left by some minor AOL 3 bugs.

However, you don't *have* to have AOL 4 to make this book useful and enjoyable. You don't even have to have Windows; plenty of the features I cover are available to Mac users as well.

WHAT YOU'LL FIND WITHIN THIS BOOK

The number one reason people sign up for an online service is to interact with others. The first four chapters—Chapter 1, *Excelling in E-Mail*, Chapter 2, *Instant Messages with Ease and Sophistication*, Chapter 3, *Wowing the Chat Room*, and Chapter 4, *Playing Premium Games*—give away the secrets of attracting like folks, repelling evil little fiends (hackers), and generally having a grand time online.

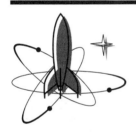

TIP

Throughout the book I refer to places—on the Web as well as on AOL—for you to check out. The latter's easy; just enter the short keyword in the Keyword/URL box. The former, though, can be a pain in the butt, especially if your typing fingers are the rebellious sort. To ease your burden, I've included all the links to Web pages discussed in the book on my Web site. Reach it by visiting the Sybex Web site at `http://www.sybex.com` and looking up *America Online Amazing Secrets* in the catalog.

The fifth chapter, *Managing AOL: Secrets to Organize By*, is a *whoa, Nellie!*—now that you've played around a bit, received some e-mail, and downloaded some files, you'll want to take a step back and make sure your hard drive is in order and still running at top speed. Files take room, and you don't want to sacrifice your sanity and quality of computing just to keep them around. Here I show you the tricks of the organizing trade.

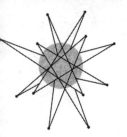

Introduction

The next few chapters—Chapter 6, *Searching with Purpose*, Chapter 7, *Hunting for Bargains and Free Stuff*, and Chapter 8, *Your Web Page*—get out there in AOL- and cyberspace to help you find what you want to find, from information to free stuff to the news you want to know, and to help you display your many talents in contests and on your homegrown Web page.

The last chapter, Chapter 9, *Accessing AOL at Home and on the Road*, helps you travel about with the confidence and connectedness you've come to expect from this modern world. I give you hints on the best ways to access AOL as well as tips to travel with.

And, of course, I sign off with an Appendix, *Help!*, which will give you all the info you'll need to figure out how to fix whatever's gone wrong.

NOTE

I've organized this book based on what I think you'll want to explore from start to finish, but you can use it just as easily as a reference manual; I explain procedures thoroughly when they come up and point you to relevant discussions in other chapters when necessary.

CONVENTIONS USED IN THIS BOOK

I use italics for emphasis and bold for anything you'll need to type in. Keywords, for instance, are the words you'll need to type into the Keyword/URL box in order to get to an AOL area. So I've placed them in bold (as in keyword **keyword**).

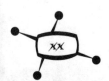

Conventions Used in This Book

I also make liberal use of Note, Tip, Warning, and Secret boxes. Notes are little asides about a subject, Tips are information you should know about the subject at hand, and Warnings (as Robot B-9 would say) call out "Danger, danger, Will Robinson!" (You, dear readers, are the Will Robinsons of the AOL world.) And while this whole book is really about the advanced stuff you can do with AOL, there are some secrets that are more secretive than others; I enclose these in the Secret boxes.

As more secrets unfold, I'll add them to my Web site, which, as I've said, you can access through http://www.sybex.com. I hope you enjoy the book as much as I enjoyed writing it. My screen name appears throughout the book, but let me just say here, I'd love to hear from you. Drop me a line at LArendal@aol.com.

Onward to online heights you never imagined possible!

Chapter

1

Excelling in E-Mail

E-mail: everyone wants it. Staying in touch with people is the number one reason people sign up for Internet service. Easier than handwriting a letter, more practical than picking up a phone, communicating via e-mail is quick and cost-effective.

In this chapter I'll speed you from the absolute basics of e-mail to the most secretive of secrets.

BONING UP ON THE BASICS

I'm going to sprint through some basic e-mail concepts to give the neophyte secret-seekers among you a solid base in e-mail.

WHAT YOU GET

After you sign up for AOL, you'll be personally welcomed—via e-mail—by the prez himself, Steve Case, as well as by the AOL

Help VP, Keith Jenkins. Figure 1.1 shows you your basic mailbox. Or rather, my basic mailbox.

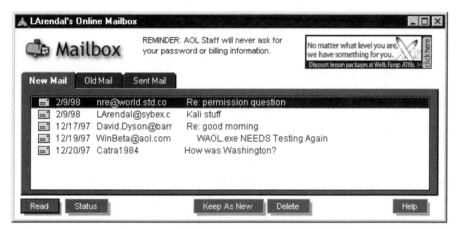

FIGURE 1.1: Your online mailbox is your temporary storage spot for mail.

From here you can read your mail (highlight the message and click Read—or just double-click the message), check when exactly your AOL friends sent their e-mails to you and when your AOL friends read your e-mails to them (Status), keep e-mail you've read in this box (Keep As New), delete mail you don't want (uh, Delete), and get help if you need it (Help).

SECRET

Notice that if you right-click on a message (while still in the Online Mailbox) you have another option: Ignore. With Ignore, your mail will be marked as read, though you haven't touched it (well, only a little) and will disappear from your Online Mailbox. Ignore is extra-useful for those meeting minutes you'll need to reference later but don't really want to delve into at the moment.

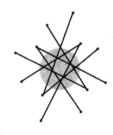

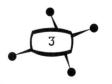

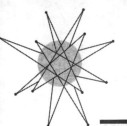

Downloads and Hotlinks—Danger, Danger, Will Robinson!

I'll talk about the how-tos of attachments later, but let me caution you right now to be very careful about e-mail with attachments. I can't emphasize this enough: never download an attachment from someone you don't know! It's okay to read the e-mail, though it will most likely be provocative ("I heard a rumor about you...You can take advantage of this great software deal...Check out this picture of me sunbathing..."). Don't be tempted to download the attached file: The evil denizens that lurk around the periphery of happy AOL Land may be sending you viruses, password-revealing programs, and whatever else they've thought of!

Just as evil takes many forms, so do password-stealers. If someone you don't know sends you an e-mail with a hotlink, don't be tempted by it. If you click it, you might be dumped onto a Web site that uses Java code to steal your password or wreak havoc on your system.

A quick look at the Old Mail tab will show you what you've read within the last few days. After it vanishes from your Online Mailbox, you'll still be able to find it in your Personal Filing Cabinet (PFC)—as long as you've set your mail preferences to retain your mail in your PFC. I talk more about that in *Have Mail Your Way* later in this chapter.

The Sent Mail tab is a little more interesting. Here's where you get to Unsend an e-mail if you have that horrified "I can't believe I said that!" realization in the morning. Of course,

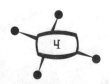

 Unsend only works if the mail was AOL-bound in the first place *and* if the recipient hasn't yet read it. (AOL's good, but a brain surgeon it is not.)

N♁TE

Old mail can be kept in your Online Mailbox for one to seven days, which I will talk about later in this chapter. Also, your mailbox will only hold 550 messages, so remember: save early and save often. I delve into your PFC in detail in Chapter 5, *Managing AOL: Secrets to Organize By*.

WARNING

If you want to Unsend an e-mail that was mailed to several people at once, you'll only be able to do so if *all* the recipients were at AOL addresses and *no one* has read it.

TIP

Unsend will delete the e-mail you've designated to Unsend from your Online Mailbox as well—but only after you close out of your Online Mailbox. If you want to preserve your words and rework them, Unsend the mail, then—while you're still in the Sent Mail tab—open the mail and copy the text to a fresh Write Mail window. Now you can close out of the Online Mailbox and watch the old version disappear forever.

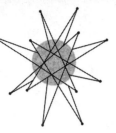

AND WHAT YOU GIVE

Now that you've mastered getting your mail, let's move on to writing and sending e-mails.

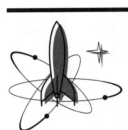

TIP

One of the cool things about the fun mail activities in this chapter is that you can do most of them from here on out offline. So if you want to log off, feel free.

To do the e-pal thing, click Write in the toolbar

and you've pulled out a piece of electronic stationery. How to work this particular type of stationery is mostly self-explanatory, as illustrated in Figure 1.2; put your correspondent's address in the Send To field, any copy recipients in the Copy To field, the subject of your letter you know where, and then chat away in that big empty box.

Of course, if you're responding to someone's message, you'll just need to hit Reply, and her address will automatically appear in the Send To field.

I'll get into attachments later on in this chapter (*Secrets of the Successfully Attached*).

For even more functionality to your text, right-click on the text box for a pop-up menu chock full of cool stuff. A lot of the options are mimicked in and more easily accessed from the Write Mail toolbar, but two extras are worth mentioning: Insert Text File and Insert Background Image.

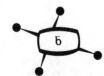

Write Mail

Send To:	nre@world.std.com	Copy To:	

Send Now

Subject: class + hanging out

Arial 10 **B** *I* U

Hey Natalie,

Did you go to class this week? Did she say anything about the test?

In other news, we're hanging out at Jupiter tonight--join us, bring Myron, come play! We'll be there around 9.

Laura

Send Later

Address Book

Mail Extras

Attachments   ☐ Request "Return Receipt" from AOL members   Help

FIGURE 1.2: Faster than a speeding fountain pen, more powerful than a transcontinental stamp, able to leap tall postal workers in a single bound

Font...
Text
Justification
Text Color...
Background Color...
Insert a Picture...
Background Picture...
Insert Text File...
Insert a Hyperlink...
Spell Check
Undo
Cut
Copy
Paste
Delete
Select All

Insert Text File will enable you to do exactly that; insert a TXT file that you wish to copy into your e-mail. Background Picture allows you to artfully place a BMP, GIF, ART, or JPG file into your e-mail—and then type or place pictures over it. (Once you insert a background image, the right-click menu will suddenly acquire a Clear Background command, which will, as you might suspect, delete the background art; kind of an artsy Undo.)

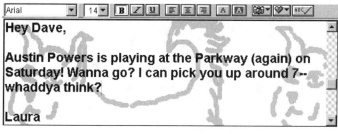

Arial 14 **B** *I* U

Hey Dave,

Austin Powers is playing at the Parkway (again) on Saturday! Wanna go? I can pick you up around 7-- whaddya think?

Laura

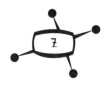

7

THE BLIND COPY SECRET

Here's a little secret: to blind copy someone—say your surprise-party cohorts as you're setting up a date with the unsuspecting surprise-party guest—put parentheses around each address you want to conceal from the message's primary recipients in the Copy To field: (screenname1, screenname2,...). See *Addressing Hints* for more about Blind Copies.

Blind copy is also extremely useful if you send a monthly newsletter out to all the members of your aikido dojo (for instance), but not everyone wants their e-mail address publicized. Blind copy also eliminates the long header your recipients would otherwise have to suffer through when you send an e-mail to a large number of people. To blind copy a group, choose the group name from the Address Book and click the Blind Copy button; each recipient will only see her name in the Send To field.

EMBEDDING ORIGINAL MESSAGES IN YOUR RESPONSE

If you excitedly read an e-mail and then just hit the Reply button, the message you're responding to will disappear, and then you'll end up explaining what you're referring to each time you write something. Annoying, yes?

But it doesn't have to be this way; you can intercalate with the best of them by taking one easy step: Highlight the part of the message you want to appear in your reply, *then* hit Reply. By penning your well-thought-out responses directly after your correspondent's statements, you can realize the conversational

quality of e-mail, which is quite different from the series of monologues that are hand written letters.

Now, if you want to intercalate the hip and easily readable

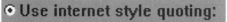

⊙ **Use internet style quoting:**
>This is an example
>of internet style quoting

way, go to Mail Center ➤ Mail Preferences and select Use Internet Style Quoting. Angle brackets (otherwise known as "greater than" symbols) will appear before each line of the original message. Your response will be unbracketed and therefore easy to distinguish from the original message.

TIP

If you resize your Write Mail window (or any window, for that matter) to a shape you'd like to make permanent, just click Window ➤ Remember Window Size Only (or Remember Window Size and Position, if such is your desire).

USING COLORFUL MAIL FRILLS

You can easily create all kinds of special effects in your mail messages with background colors, text colors, and font selection, as I point out in Figure 1.3.

Be warned; if your pen pal is somewhere in that vast expanse of Internet space, he won't be able to see the fun things you do to your mail; only AOL users can fully take advantage of the artsy e-mail tools at your disposal.

However, appreciation is not won easily, even from fellow AOLies. Think long and hard before you send your decorated missive; is it readable or does it rival *Wired*'s pages? Is pink on purple appropriate for a note to your boss? Is your recipient particularly crabby about unnecessary special effects (and do you want to push that button)?

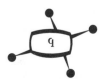

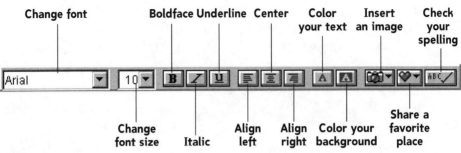

FIGURE 1.3: A plethora of decorative tools await your artistic touch.

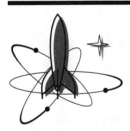

TIP

Speaking of Mail Frills, have you clicked the Mail Center's Fun with Mail button? From here you can find online postcards, newsletters and more little surprises that AOL has thoughtfully provided for your e-mailing pleasure.

E-Mail Art

You can create art in your Write Mail window just by using the color tools available in the message-box toolbar.

NOTE

Don't try to send art in a message over the Internet! It won't work, and your recipient will feel cheated. The artistic method described here is strictly for AOL-to-AOL communication.

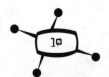

However, drawing a picture in your Write Mail window is a bit laborious. Painting a picture with a graphics program (and then inserting—with the Insert a Picture button—or attaching the image) is a lot easier. That said, drawing in AOL's message window is one of those obscure things you'll want to say you know how to do. Really, you'll be proud of yourself.

So say you've just moved to a little pueblo in Sante Fe, New Mexico (it's hypothetical; work with me here). Even before your photos are developed and scanned in, you can draw a little picture, like the one in Figure 1.4, in your "Hey, I've Got a New Snail Mail Address" e-mail.

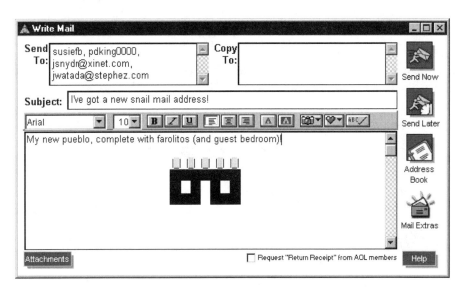

FIGURE 1.4:   You can be quite picturesque in your e-mail.

Here's how I created this dwelling:

1. Open up a Write Mail window.

2. Create the basic shape (a rectangle in this example) using underlines (just tapping the Spacebar won't do it).

3. Highlight the shape and, using the Background Color button, select the background color you want.

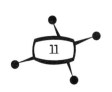

4. Add features. Pipes (the vertical lines) can become the vertical parts of window frames and doors.

5. Highlight the features and underlines and color as desired with the Text Color button.

Serious Font Fun

In certain fonts you can hold down the Ctrl or Alt button and access little snippets of art the font creators hid. Or, even better, you can install fonts that *are* art. The possibilities that come to mind are endless. But remember, if you use a font of this type, your recipient must have that font to view your picture properly.

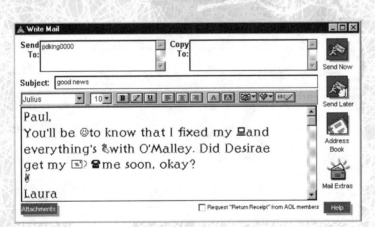

Make a rebus with Wingdings

MORE ART TOOLS

After you've mastered drawing with squares, you'll be delighted to know that you have a graphics program on your computer already. In Windows 95's Paint (Start ➤ Programs ➤ Accessories ➤ Paint), you can draw to your heart's content, save your picture as a

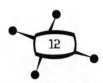

BMP file, and then insert the image right in your message window using the Insert a Picture button.

Even More Art Tools

You can also add pictures from the Picture Gallery to your e-mail messages:

1. Open a Write Mail window.

2. From AOL's menu bar, choose File ➤ Open Picture Gallery.

3. In the Directory box on the left, navigate to a folder with BMP, ART, GIF, and/or JPG files and click on Open Gallery.

NOTE

Notice the Capture Picture button at the bottom of the Picture Gallery; you'll need to install a digital camera to use this option.

4. As you see in Figure 1.5, you'll see a thumbnail of each piece of art. To choose one, select it and drag and drop it to your Write Mail text field. Alternatively, click it once and select the Insert in E-Mail button.

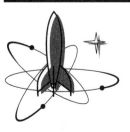

TIP

To edit a gallery item, click on it and, in the ensuing window, click the little down arrow at top left. A brave new toolbar will present itself to you, allowing you to manipulate the picture in all sorts of ways.

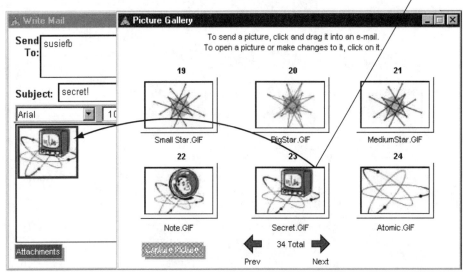

FIGURE 1.5: Not the Smithsonian, but a gallery nonetheless

ADDRESSING HINTS

A couple of things you should note; instead of laboriously remembering and then laboriously typing your friends' e-mail addresses into the Send To field, just store their addresses in your Address book, shown in Figure 1.6. You can easily address future messages by calling up stored addresses, as I'll show you.

ADDING FRIENDS

I'll get into making friends later, but for now let's concentrate on the friends you already have. To add people to your Address book, follow these steps:

1. Click the Address Book button on the right side of your Write Mail window.

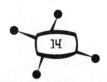

2. In the Address Book window, click either New Person or New Group.

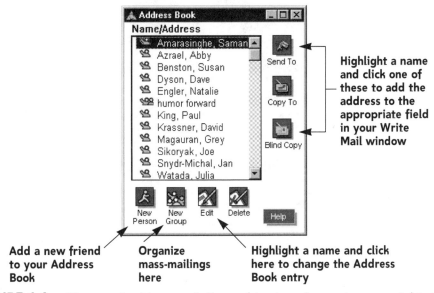

Highlight a name and click one of these to add the address to the appropriate field in your Write Mail window

Add a new friend to your Address Book

Organize mass-mailings here

Highlight a name and click here to change the Address Book entry

FIGURE 1.6: The e-mail addresses of all your friends and acquaintances, right at your mouse tip.

NOTE

Which category you pick depends on what you want to accomplish. If you want to send mail to an individual, you'll want New Person. If you're in the habit of sending one message to a bunch of people—for instance, a yearly update to your widely dispersed group of college friends— you'll want to pick New Group.

3. If you are adding an individual, fill in the fields in the New Person box as labeled (see Figure 1.7). If you want to remember something about your friend, use the Notes section. Birthdays, anniversaries, odd habits...

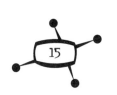

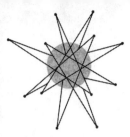

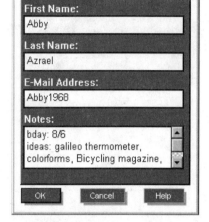

FIGURE 1.7: The important stuff to know: name, e-mail address, birthday...

4. If you have a scanned photo of your friend, you can place it in the Picture tab (click the Picture tab, then click Select Picture and then root around for the ART, BMP, JPG, or GIF file on your hard drive).

5. When you're done, click OK.

SECRET

If you have a picture that isn't one of the usual files (ART, BMP, JPG, or GIF) but that you want to add to your Address Book, you can open the file in question with Imaging for Windows 95 (Start ➤ Programs ➤ Accessories ➤ Imaging) and save it as a BMP (using Save As, of course). Alternatively, you can open it with AOL: click File ➤ Open, double-click the image file, and click File ➤ Save As to save it as a GIF, BMP, or JPG file.

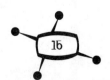

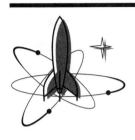

TIP

Say you're in your address book (for whatever reason) and you see the name of someone you owe a letter to. Just double-click the name to open up a Write Mail window with that person already entered into the Send To field. What could be easier?

Adding a Group of Friends

New Group is even easier: In your Address Book, name your group something obvious (so you remember which group is which and don't send that Doom death-match challenge to your azalea-growers club). And then list the addresses of each of the group members, separated by commas or returns.

Address Tricks

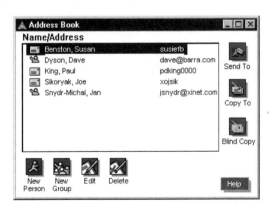

What if your business partner has two e-mail addresses, and you want to send messages to both addresses almost all of the time? (She travels a lot, and you're never sure which address she'll be accessing next.) You can't have two e-mail addresses in one Address Book entry, but you can have multiple entries that use the exact same name. If you expand your address book (drag the right edge out), you can see the address each name is assigned to. In that way you can decide which to use if you have two or more entries for the same person.

17

THE NEW GROUP/MULTIPLE RECIPIENT SECRET:

You knew there had to be an easier way to fill out your New Group list than typing all those addresses in again. If you want to create an Address Book group and you've already got the addresses in your Address Book:

1. Go to Mail Center ➤ Address Book and double-click the first name you wish to add to your new group. A Write Mail window will come up with that person's address in the Send To field. (Don't worry, it's all part of the plan.)

2. Now go back to the Address Book (Window ➤ Address Book) and continue to double-click the rest of the names you want in your group. These two steps will give you your multiple-recipient e-mail; to make these multitudes a permanent group, read on.

3. When you've got everybody, highlight the names in the Write Mail window's Send To field and copy (Ctrl+C).

4. Switch back to the Address Book, click the New Group button to bring up the New Group dialog box, place your cursor in the Addresses field, and paste (Ctrl+V).

5. Click OK, and you're done!

You can now delete the Write Mail window—unless you have something to send your group of pals.

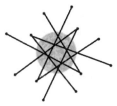

Alternatively, you can use the name fields to keep e-mail addresses straight. Just type in the person's name and a brief description of which e-mail address you've assigned, such as *Alison at work* and *Alison at home* (not *Alison1* and *Alison2*).

New Address Book entries →

Old Address Book entries →

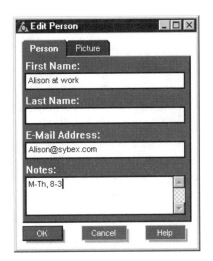

Keep in mind, though, only 19 characters in all (including the comma that separates the last name from the first) will show up in your address book. If you do choose to differentiate between addresses in this way, type everything into the first name field (or last name field—AOL isn't picky) to maximize the characters that will show up in the Address Book proper.

SETTING UP FAMILY MEMBERS—OR PERSONAS

One excellent way to protect your good name is to not use it in public places. And most of AOL is pretty darn public! If you want to subscribe to a newsgroup or chat idly (and even if you want to chat with purpose), consider doing it under a separate name.

As an AOLie, you're allowed five names on your account. One's already taken up by your master account screen name, the name you chose that happy day you opened your AOL account. You know, the one that gets the monthly bill. So you've got four slots left to do with as you please.

NOTE

Well, "as you please" isn't entirely true. Your name has to be PG-rated, plus you can't use any restricted words—like *net*—in a name. You can be as silly, cutesy, or serious as you like, though. Lurk a bit, and you'll see all types of names floating around AOL.

To add a screen name (or two or three):

1. First, make sure you are logged on as the master account.

2. From the toolbar, choose My AOL ➤ Screen Names.

3. Click Create a Screen Name.

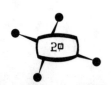

Why You Should Have at Least Two Screen Names

Don't underestimate the importance of using an alias for your public pursuits. Newsgroup messages (no small potatoes, these!) will collect only in your alias' mailbox, and unsavory characters (who get your name from your Member Profile and by other, more obscure means) will send unwanted messages and files to your alias' mailbox. Your friends will send heartfelt and sincere messages to the box held by your master account screen name. In this way, you'll know which mail to read and which to idly riffle through!

4. Type your new screen name into the text box and press Create a Screen Name.

5. If AOL approves, you'll need to decide on a password. (If it doesn't, a dialog box will notify you of such and allow you to choose another name.)

6. Finally, you'll need to designate an age group for this name. If it's your kid, you'll want to select Kids Only, Young Teen (ages 13-15), or Mature Teen (ages 15-18). If it's your alter ego, you'll want to select 18+.

NOTE

If you've come up with a new moniker you want to use but you already have five names, click Delete a Screen Name to purge yourself of one of them.

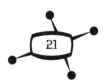

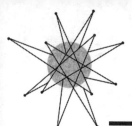

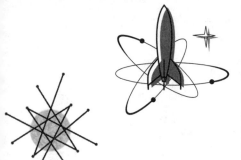

TIP

No one else will be able to use a deleted screen name for six months after you hit that OK to Delete button. If you think better of your decision to trash a name, you can reconstitute it within the 6-month period by going to My AOL ➤ Screen Names ➤ Restore a Screen Name, highlighting your long-lost screen name, and clicking the Recover button.

YOUR MAIL IN A FLASH (OR YOUR MONEY BACK)

Now that you've mastered basic e-mail, you can manage it efficiently by automating it. Formerly called Flashsessions, Auto AOL can—without you even so much as pressing a button—log on, send your prewritten messages and newsgroup and message board postings, download your mail and file attachments, and log off. All in minutes, depending on how cutting edge your modem is. And then you are free to wake up, groggily make your way to the computer, and read your e-mail offline. At your leisure. This hour or next.

NOTE

Auto AOL is the e-equivalent of your computer putting on snowboots and earmuffs, shoveling the path to your mailbox, picking up your letters, throwing your written correspondence in, flipping the flag, and trudging back inside (removing the boots before entering, of course). (Those of you who live in buildings with those groovy mail chutes up to the 50th floor, I can only say: I'm jealous.)

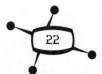

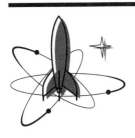

TIP

If you are not a surfer or information-gatherer but your friends have scattered to the decidedly rounded corners of the globe, the most inexpensive AOL service, which comes with just a few hours of online time a month, combined with Auto AOL message retrieval and posting, is for you. If all you do with AOL is done offline (such as reading and writing e-mail), your Auto AOL sessions shouldn't exceed the allotted hours under the limited access agreement. To change your pricing plan, go to Help ➤ Accounts and Billing. Read about your options under AOL Pricing Plans (in the right-hand box), and change your options under Change Billing Method or Price Plan (on the left).

To set up your Automatic AOL sessions, choose Mail Center ➤ Set Up Automatic AOL. Auto AOL setup is pretty self-explanatory (I'll fill in whatever gaps there are right here), so bypass the walkthrough (you'll only get the walkthrough screen the first time you set up Auto AOL anyway) and go straight to Expert Setup.

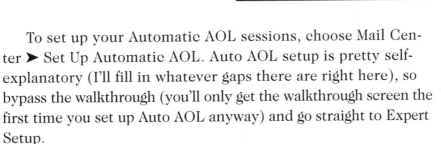

In the Automatic AOL window (shown in Figure 1.8):

1. Choose Select Names to select the screen names you want to schedule automatic mail retrieval for. Check the box next to the name that is to receive the benefits of this service, then type that screen name's password into the password box in the right column. This action will store your password for AOL's automatic retrieval. Repeat as desired.

Screen Name	Password
☑ LArendal	*****

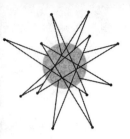

2. In the Auto AOL setup box shown in Figure 1.8, select the procedures you want to automate. Unfortunately, all the screen names that get automatic mail will have to suffer with the same choices. I heartily recommend the first two choices, Send Mail and Get Unread Mail. I also recommend the fourth and fifth choices, Send Postings (to newsgroups) and Get Unread Postings. The Download Files Marked to Be Downloaded Later option is also quite safe, as these are files you've found in your perusal of AOL's offerings and have marked to retrieve. This option will not allow AOL to automatically download files attached to incoming e-mail, only those you've okayed to put on your hard drive.

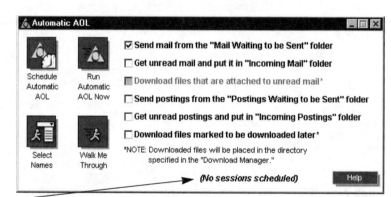

If you schedule regular AutoAOL sessions, check this line to make sure the sessions have been enabled.

FIGURE 1.8:   Your setup-automation window

WARNING

I counsel against enabling the third Auto AOL option, Download Files Attached to Unread Mail. If you can't see your mail, you don't know who sent you what, and any unknown downloads could carry viruses. In addition, if the download is unwanted *and* huge, you might be paying for wasted time.

NOTE

Now that you've told Auto AOL exactly what to automate, you can choose to set it up to run without you (as I detail in Step 3) or you can run it manually whenever you want to retrieve the items you told it to in Step 2. To run Auto AOL manually, ignore Step 3 and, from AOL's menu bar, choose Mail Center ➤ Run Auto AOL Now ➤ Begin.

3. Now that you've got Who and What in place, you can schedule your sessions by clicking Schedule Automatic AOL. In the Schedule Automatic AOL dialog box that appears, you have all sorts of options, so go to town.

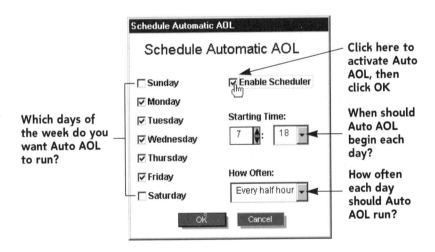

Which days of the week do you want Auto AOL to run?

Click here to activate Auto AOL, then click OK

When should Auto AOL begin each day?

How often each day should Auto AOL run?

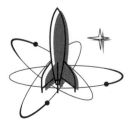

TIP

Remember, though, when you schedule your Auto AOL, just clicking OK is *not* enough. You must activate the scheduler by checking the Enable Scheduler box at the top of the window.

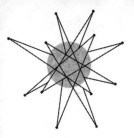

Remember, to run Auto AOL automatically, your computer must be on and the AOL software must be running (in other words, you'll want the Sign On—or Goodbye from America Online—screen up on your computer).

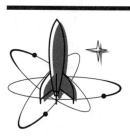

TIP

Even if you've set up Auto AOL sessions to run automatically, you can still run them manually whenever you want (Mail Center ➤ Run Auto AOL Now ➤ Begin).

Automatic Drawbacks

Oh, to everything there is a drawback. Auto AOL can tie up phone lines; that 4 am call from Cousin Mai from Japan can get pretty screwed up when Auto AOL breaks in to retrieve your mail.

The other big, big drawback is that to automate e-mail retrieval you have to store your password (as you did in Step 1), and that innocent-looking e-mail from a stranger with an attached "sexy picture taken at the beach" could instead be a hacker virus that will detect your stored password(s) and automatically e-mail them back to the villain himself. That is, if you fall for the bait. Consider yourself warned.

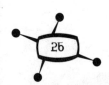

CHECKING MAIL FROM ANOTHER COMPUTER

So you're visiting Uncle Kim in San Francisco, and you suddenly remember that your best Frenchwoman Martine was going to let you know—via e-mail—whether or not she'd accepted your proposal. You don't have to fly back to New York to log onto your account! Just log onto your account using the AOL software on Uncle Kim's computer.

How?

1. In the Sign On screen, click the drop-down arrow next to Select Screen Name and select Guest.

2. Click Sign On; the modem will do its screeching thing, and you'll be asked to enter your account info: screen name and password.

3. You're on!

You can check your incoming mail (mail you haven't yet read, which therefore still resides on AOL's computers), send mail (telling Martine you accept her counterproposal and will be joining her in France next week), and everything else that doesn't require your hard drive (for instance, you can't check your Personal Filing Cabinet). Best of all, your account—not Uncle Kim's—will be billed.

NOTE

Of course, any files you download will end up on Uncle Kim's hard drive, so if you receive anything groovy or find anything you must have during your AOL session, put it on hold through the Download Later option and wait until you're home to make it yours.

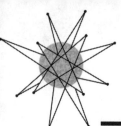

SECRET

You can check your non–AOL-account mail (for instance, from your work computer) from AOL for Windows 95. Go to keyword **telnet** to learn how.

SECRETS OF THE SUCCESSFULLY ATTACHED

Attachments in AOL 4 and beyond are a wonder and a joy. Beginning with AOL 4, you can attach as many documents as you want to your e-mail (AOL 3 and earlier only allow one attachment per e-mail). This fact alone finally makes AOL viable for business purposes.

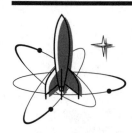

TIP

You will want to attach document files over 32K to your e-mail messages rather than including them in your mail message. You'll also want to attach formatted documents to be absolutely sure the formatting survives the journey.

To attach a document to your e-mail, click the Attachments button in the Write Mail window. In the resulting Attachments window:

1. Click the Attach button to get into Explorer and find the file you wish to attach.

2. When you've found the file, double-click it.

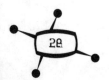

3. If you want to attach more files (say from different folders) to the message, repeat the above steps.

4. When you're satisfied with your selection, click OK to get back to your e-mail message.

DETACHING FROM E-MAILS YOU WRITE

If you're going merrily about your business, attaching files willy-nilly, writing happily away, and suddenly realize that you don't want to send Aunt Malanctha's letter to your business partner, AOL has the solution for you.

To detach a file you've already attached to your e-mail, click Attachments once more (if you're not already in the Attachment window), highlight the offending file, and click Detach.

DETACHING FROM E-MAILS YOU'VE RECEIVED

So you've received an e-mail from a friend; you notice that before you double-click it, it looks like an envelope with a floppy disk lurking behind it. When you open up the e-mail, you see only the words *Read Me!* and some download options. (This

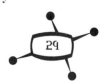

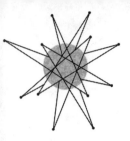

scenario is directly opposite from that of receiving an e-mail with an attachment from someone you *don't* know, which is an e-mail you should just delete. See my earlier rants on this subject…)

Detaching the document is easy; when you open up the e-mail only to see the words *Read Me!*, as I've done in Figure 1.9, you'll see three extra buttons at the bottom of the window: Download Now, Download Later, and Delete. (If you're offline, Download Now will be inactive.) Choose whichever you're inclined to; Download Now will immediately tie up your AOL software (if it's a small file, it'll be less than a minute), and Download Later will tie it up later.

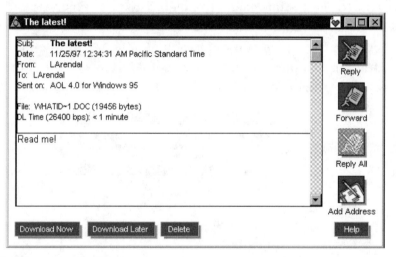

FIGURE 1.9:   Download me!

ENCODING: MAKING SENSE OF SCRAMBLED FILES

AOL attachments are automatically encoded using MIME (multi-purpose Internet mail extensions). A lot of e-mail programs will, at the recipient's end, detect MIME and automatically unencrypt your mail, allowing your correspondent to read English rather than Machine.

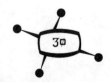

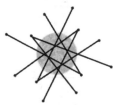

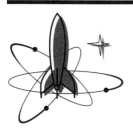

TIP

Remember where you downloaded your file to. Once downloaded, it's somewhere on your hard drive, waiting for you to find it (AOL's default download directory is c:\AOL\Download, but you might have changed that during the download process). If you completely space where you put it, choose from the toolbar: My Files ➤ Download Manager ➤ Show Files Downloaded, highlight the file you want to find, and click Show Status. The third line shows you the pathname you'll have to follow to find your file.

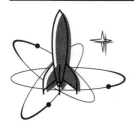

TIP

If your friend's e-mail program doesn't automatically unencrypt your attachments, have her search the Internet for Wincode freeware.

AOL doesn't unencrypt some encryptions (including MIME from some mail programs), so you might get some attachments you can't make heads nor tails of. Don't despair:

 If the file extension is .MME (MIME-encoded), download VB40032.DLL and VBRUN300.DLL (search for Visual Basic Runtime) from the AOL software library. When you double-click on the file, it will automatically be unencrypted. If you're still having trouble, download Wincode from keyword **mime**; after you register it, you can use it to manually unencrypt any problematic files.

 If the file's extension is .UUE or the first line of the file mentions "begin *filename*.txt" (meaning it's Uuencoded), download Stuffit Expander for

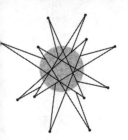

Windows from the AOL software library. When you double-click on the .UUE file, Stuffit will automatically unencrypt *and* decompress it.

If the extension is HQX or mentions BinHex in the first line of the file (therefore, it's been BinHexed), download Stuffit Expander for Windows from the AOL software library. When you double-click on the HQX file, Stuffit will automatically unencrypt and decompress it.

COMPRESSION AND SPEEDY ATTACHMENTS

The best way to send files is to compress them before you attach them. Compression programs take out all the redundancies (redundant characters and formatting commands), leaving trace codes so the redundancies can be put back in when a mere mortal wants to see the file. Without redundancies, the file will sail smoothly and quickly over the wires; you and your friends will be grateful for the comparatively short upload and download times.

NOTE

You'll want to make sure your recipients have a decompression program—such as PKZip, WinZip, Stuffit—that matches yours.

WinZip is an easy shareware compression program to download and try out. See Chapter 7, *Hunting for Bargains and Free Stuff,* for details on finding cool shareware on AOL and the Internet.

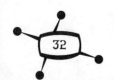

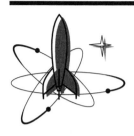

TIP

After downloading a compressed file (for instance, one with a .zip extension), just sign off from AOL; your file will be automatically decompressed.

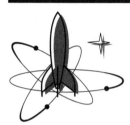

TIP

If you attach more than one file to your e-mail, AOL will automatically compress it with WinZip. Whether or not he has WinZip, your recipient will be able to double-click on the zipped file he receives and decompress your offerings.

Encouraging Creativity and Shareware

I read a thought-provoking statement about shareware the other day; shareware only works if the average shareware consumer pays for it, and *you* are the average shareware consumer. If you think you don't have to pay for it because someone else will, probably no one else will. If you think paying for shareware is a great way to reward smart individuals who just want a ten-spot for their effort, and you pay for it, probably most others will too.

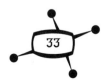

FTP: The Lengthy Secret to Sharing Lengthy Files

For big file transfers, consider FTP. As an AOL member, you have 2MB of online space per screen name, which you can use for a groovy Web site or for file transfer via FTP—or both.

To upload a file to your FTP space:

1. From the toolbar choose Internet ➤ FTP (File Transfer).

NOTE

FTP stands for file transfer protocol, which basically means the structure within which you can exchange files.

Go To
FTP

2. Choose Go to FTP.

3. Scroll down the Favorite Sites list and double-click members.aol.com.

4. You'll be connected to FTP and offered some introductory information; click OK.

5. Click the Upload button.

6. Create a name for the file; if you're an author FTP'ing a chapter to your publisher (for instance), you'll probably want to name it something like *BookTitleChapter1*. The default file type—binary—is most likely the one you want. When you're satisfied, click Continue.

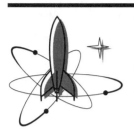

TIP

If you're uploading confidential files, or you simply don't want just anyone to have access to the files on your FTP site, place the uploaded files in the Private folder. Anyone who needs a file from you will have to know the exact path and file name in order to access and download it. Casual browsers will see no files listed on your FTP site.

NOTE

Letters, numbers, periods, hyphens, and underscores are okay in FTP file names. Spaces are not allowed.

7. To target the file you want to share, click the Select File button. Browse your hard drive and, when you find it, double-click the file.

8. Check the file name in FTP's Upload File window to make doubly sure you got the right one. When you're ready, click Send.

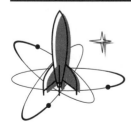

TIP

If you're dissatisfied with the name (you suddenly realize it was Chapter 2 you uploaded), click Utilities and Rename it. Or, if you decide you're not quite ready to let go of the file, click Utilities and Delete it.

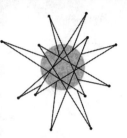

Now you can send a message off to your publisher telling her that Chapter 1 can be downloaded by FTP'ing to members.aol.com, typing **cd../*YourScreenName*/** and downloading *Book-TitleChapter1*. (For instance, my FTP message would be "type **cd../LArendal/** and download AmericaOnlineAmazing-SecretsChapter1.")

NOTE

If the person receiving your file is also an AOL member, she can easily retrieve your file by clicking on Internet (in the toolbar) ➤ FTP ➤ Go to FTP, selecting the Other Site button, and typing **member:/screenname** (such as **member:/larendal**) into the Other Site Address text field. She will then be able to access your public files.

FTP FILES BACKATCHA

If your publisher has any comments (such as *great chapter!* or *good point!*), she might want to send the file back to you so you can see the comments. Before she can FTP the file back to you, you will need to create an Incoming folder in your */YourScreen-Name* directory. To do so:

1. Navigate to your FTP space (from the toolbar, click Internet ➤ FTP ➤ Go to FTP ➤ members.aol.com), which will look like mine, members.aol.com:/LArendal shown in Figure 1.10, but with your screen name on it.

2. Click the Create Directory button.

3. Type **incoming** in the resulting dialog box, click Continue, and then click OK.

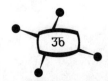

4. Repeat if you want to create other directories. If not, click Cancel.

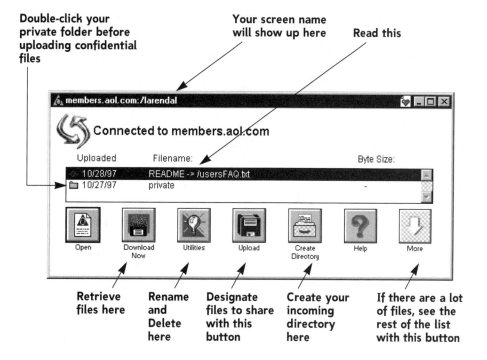

Double-click your private folder before uploading confidential files

Your screen name will show up here

Read this

Retrieve files here

Rename and Delete here

Designate files to share with this button

Create your incoming directory here

If there are a lot of files, see the rest of the list with this button

FIGURE 1.10: Except for the screen name, this is what your FTP space will look like when you access it the first time.

Others will be able to upload files for you to this directory only. (Once they do so, they'll need to tell you something's there via phone or e-mail.)

WARNING

Once you've created the Incoming folder, be sure to check back and clean it out every so often. The 2MB limit applies to everything that's in your FTP directory, and K's can pile up fast.

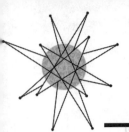

FTP: Dangerous Fun?

You'll certainly have noticed by now that you have access to other FTP sites, some of which contain groovy programs. Be warned, though, AOL doesn't guarantee these files against viruses, so it's safer to use AOL's software libraries.

That aside, you can sure find some fun stuff!

TIP

If you want to check out an FTP site, you don't have to burrow all the way into FTP land to get to it; just type **ftp://ftp.site.name** into the Keyword/URL box and click Go. AOL's Web browser will take you there.

HAVE MAIL YOUR WAY

Just as you can customize the way your messages look, you can customize how your mailbox runs with Mail Preferences and with Mail Controls.

MAIL PREFERENCES

To get to Mail Preferences, choose Mail Center ➤ Mail Preferences (Figure 1.11). Here you can organize your Online Mailbox. The most useful options are highlighted on the following pages.

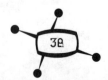

Mail Preferences

☐ Confirm mail after it has been sent
☑ Close mail after it has been sent
☑ Confirm when mail is marked to send later
☐ Retain all mail I send in my Personal Filing Cabinet
☑ Retain all mail I read in my Personal Filing Cabinet
☐ Perform a spell check before sending mail
☑ Use white mail headers
☐ Show addresses as hyperlinks
○ Use AOL style quoting: ◉ Use internet style quoting:

    <<This is an example   >This is an example
    of AOL style quoting>>   >of internet style quoting

You must be online to change your "old mail" preferences.

[OK]   [Cancel]

FIGURE 1.11: Your choices, gentle readers...

Save the Mails!

There's one very important thing you'll want to make sure you
do with your mail: store the messages you want to keep.

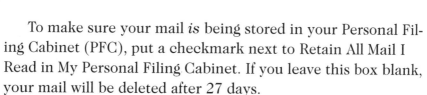

WARNING

Mail archival is *not* a default; you must choose it—or lose
your mail messages forever.

To make sure your mail *is* being stored in your Personal Filing Cabinet (PFC), put a checkmark next to Retain All Mail I
Read in My Personal Filing Cabinet. If you leave this box blank,
your mail will be deleted after 27 days.

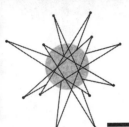

NOTE

Keep in mind that when stored in your PFC, your mail is hanging out on your hard drive, and hard drives get cranky and sluggish when full. I'll talk more about the PFC in Chapter 5, but for now just remember to organize your mail and clean it out once in a while. Remember to delete messages you don't want before you even read them, lest they clutter your PFC unnecessarily.

Auto Spellcheck

Another option that I think is super-useful is the automatic spellcheck; if this option is enabled and you click Send (whether Now or Later), AOL will automatically launch the Check Spelling dialog box. Yes, you have a spellcheck button in your Write Mail window toolbar (and it works exactly the same way), but if you forget to use it, dictating an automatic spellcheck in your Preferences could save you some embarassment. I mean, embarrassment.

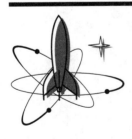

TIP

If you're a keyboarder—and you prefer to manually spellcheck only when you feel it's necessary—your short-cut to the Check Spelling box is Ctrl+=. And if you're a regular at the spellcheck counter, but once in a while you want to pass on it, just press the Ctrl key while you send the message.

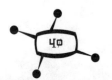

NOTE

AOL also sports an in-depth thesaurus; from the menu bar, just choose Edit ➤ Thesaurus, type the word you want to match in the text field, and click the Look Up button.

Just Say No to Confirmation Dialogs

If you hate confirmation dialog boxes (after all, you clicked Send Now—or Send Later—and the message disappeared; why do you need to see a message saying it's been sent?), uncheck the first and third options.

Click'n'Go

Show Addresses As Hyperlinks allows you to single-click on any address within the From, To, or CC fields of an e-mail to open a new Write Mail window with that address inserted in the Send To field.

Keep Unanswered Mail Visible

If you are the type that mulls over letters and responds only after several days of thought, but you like to keep unanswered messages visible so you remember to write back, you have a couple of options. Of course, you could create an *Unanswered Mail* folder in your Personal Filing Cabinet, but I bet you'd forget to check your PFC. I would.

Your options are:

  Keep As New

  Retain messages in your Old Mail tab for up to seven days

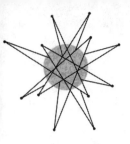

In your Online Mailbox, you can click the Keep As New button to uncheck a message you've read. In essence, you're tricking the AOL computers into thinking you haven't read it. This strategy will keep unanswered messages in your face, but if ignored too long the messages will pile up—in a big way.

Alternatively, you can specify in Mail Preferences that you wish read mail to stay in the Old Mail tab of your Online Mailbox for as few as one and as many as seven days after you've read it. This way, you can quickly check your Old Mail tab after you read your new mail. Of course, the messages in Old Mail are gonna pile up too!

MAIL CONTROLS

This area is where you take control of the gate that opens to let mail in. Cutting ties with your old roommate, especially after what he did to your favorite shirt? No problem. Want to block Internet mail to your five-year-old? Piece of cake. Or do you just want to be left alone? You can do that, too.

To get to Mail Controls:

1. First, log on with the master account screen name. This screen name is the name that set up the account with AOL, the one associated with the credit card paying the AOL bill.

2. Choose Mail Center ➤ Mail Controls.

3. Click the Go to Mail Controls button.

4. Choose the screen name you want to institute controls for.

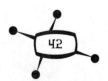

5. As you see in Figure 1.12, you have a lot of choices; control away.

6. When you're done, click OK.

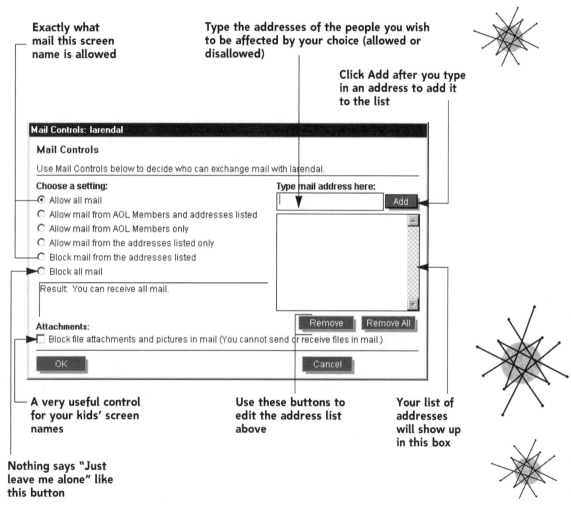

Exactly what mail this screen name is allowed

Type the addresses of the people you wish to be affected by your choice (allowed or disallowed)

Click Add after you type in an address to add it to the list

A very useful control for your kids' screen names

Use these buttons to edit the address list above

Your list of addresses will show up in this box

Nothing says "Just leave me alone" like this button

FIGURE 1.12: I can still receive all mail and attachments! Phew!

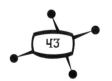

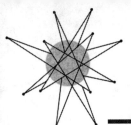

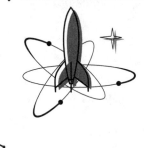

TIP

You'll notice that in the Mail Controls window, which you whip through in Step 2, you can click on the Junk Mail button on the right and find info on AOL's actions against junk mail. If—despite your attempts to control your mail—you get junkmail, just forward it to TOSSPAM. If AOL gets enough reports on an address, they'll add its domain to their list of domains that cannot send mail to AOL members. (Yes, there are addresses out there that you can't get e-mail from; like *bulkmail.net*. I snuck a look at the list, and given that my example is quite a bit more PG than most of the entries, I think we can do without 'em.)

HEY, MISTER POSTMAN

Do you want to make some e-friends? Or just get some e-mail on a topic you're interested in? Riffle through the Mail Center's Fun with Mail link in the lower right of the Mail Center window. (As always, get here by selecting Mail Center ➤ Mail Center from the AOL toolbar.)

From here you can easily join a newsgroup, sign up to receive a newsletter, get news on your topic of choice sent right to your mailbox, and more.

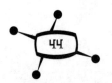

THE MESSAGE BOARD SIGNATURE SECRET

New

You can invite other message board readers to e-mail you by including a hotlink to an automatic Write Mail window in your message board signature. To set this hotlink up, go to Favorites ➤ Favorite Places and click the New button.

In the Add New Favorite Place box, select the New Favorite Place radio button, and enter the text you wish to become your hotlink (something like **e-mail me!**) in the top text field. In the bottom field, enter **mailto:*YourScreenName*@aol.com** (such as **mailto:LArendal@aol.com**). Don't forget to substitute your screen name for *YourScreenName*.

When you press OK, the new fave place will be added to your Favorite Places entries. Now, create an automatic signature for your message board postings (available on boards with a pushpin background): click the tiny Preferences button along the bottom of the window to get into your Message Board Preferences, and just drag and drop that *e-mail me!* Fave Place heart over to your Signature box. If you're on one of the older message boards (these have a plain white background and do not have automatic signature capabilities), you can achieve the same effect by dragging and dropping the heart over to each message you write (these boards will eventually be converted to the newer groovier look).

Continued

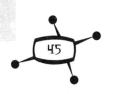

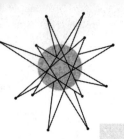

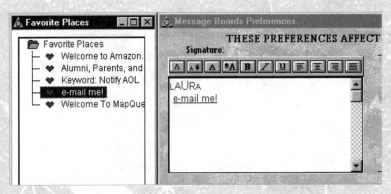

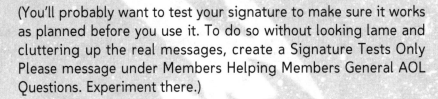

Drag 'n' drop from Fave Places to your signature area

(You'll probably want to test your signature to make sure it works as planned before you use it. To do so without looking lame and cluttering up the real messages, create a Signature Tests Only Please message under Members Helping Members General AOL Questions. Experiment there.)

Now that you've got e-mail down pat, let's turn to Instant Messages, the way to chat privately with someone in real time. Like a phone, but with spelling mistakes...

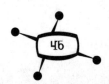

Chapter 2

Instant Messages with Ease and Sophistication

Even more immediate than e-mail, and offering more conversational confusion than the most partied-out party, instant messages—IMs to all of you in the know—offer instant-gratification communication with anyone online. Super easy to use, IMs approach the reach-out-and-touch-someone ethos of the telephone.

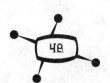

A Quick Intro to IMing

Before I get into the complexities of instant messaging, let me refresh your memory on the how-tos of IMing.

To open up a Send Instant Message window, take any of these actions:

 Press Ctrl+I.

 From the Menu bar, choose People ➤ Instant Message.

 If your Buddy List window is in view and the IM recipient of your desiring is online, select her screen name and click the IM icon. If you've taken steps to check a person out by viewing her profile and using the handy Locate button to find out whether she's online and/or in a chat room, you'll have the opportunity to send an IM (if she is indeed online).

Now that you have the Send Instant Message window open, type the recipient's screen name in the To field as shown in Figure 2.1. At that point, you can click the Available button and make sure she's online and accepting IMs (if she's turned IMs off, you won't be able to get through to her).

Now the antics begin. Type your message in the text box and, once you're satisfied, click Send to fling it across AOL space. It will pop up on your correspondent-elect's screen in an Instant Message From window. At that point she can choose to respond by clicking Respond, or she can click Cancel to get rid of it. If she chooses Cancel, you just won't hear back. If she clicks Respond, she'll have the same writing implements you do, as you see in Figure 2.2.

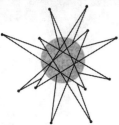

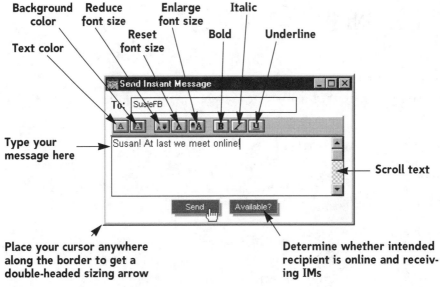

Background color **Reduce font size** **Enlarge font size** **Italic**

Reset font size **Bold** **Underline**

Text color

Type your message here

Scroll text

Place your cursor anywhere along the border to get a double-headed sizing arrow

Determine whether intended recipient is online and receiving IMs

FIGURE 2.1: The simplicity of the instant message revealed

TIP

If you resize your IM window (or any window, for that matter) to a shape you'd like to keep, just click Window ➤ Remember Window Size Only.

TIP

Instead of laboriously moving your cursor over to the Send button every time you're ready to jettison a missive, just press Ctrl+Enter or, alternatively, Tab+Spacebar.

The whole conversation is compiled here →

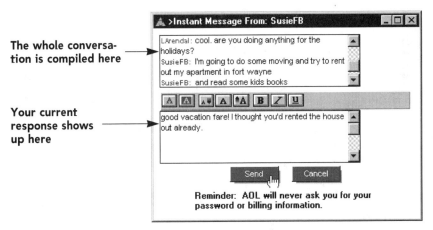

Your current response shows up here →

FIGURE 2.2: Scroll the top scrollbar to track the conversation, the bottom bar to see all of your response.

Password Scammers

Notice the reminder at the bottom of the incoming IM in Figure 2.2. A surprising number of would-be hackers pose as AOL staff and send instant messages to AOLies stating that due to software difficulties, their accounts will be terminated unless they respond with their password.

Never give your password out!

If and when you get one of these messages, highlight the text, copy it, type **TOS** into the Keyword/URL box, and click Go. At the Terms of Service window, choose Report a Violation, then click the Instant Message Notes button, and paste the text of the IM into the Paste the Solicitation Here box at the bottom of this TOS window. Go back to the offending IM and likewise copy the screen name and paste it into the password-violation Screen Name box. Then delete the IM and forget about it.

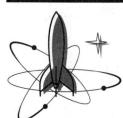

TIP

If you find you're getting a plethora of IMs clamoring for your password or credit card number, create a shortcut to the TOS Password Violation window, as detailed in *Reporting IM Harassers*.

IM Tips

Those were the basics of instant messaging; here come some fine-tuning hints.

Multitasking

If you're in the middle of something—say a particularly fascinating article on the aboveground nuclear testing experiments the US conducted in the '50s (and no, screaming WE'RE ALL GOING TO DIE in your instant message is not the tip I had in mind here)—you may find you've partially or completely obscured your instant message window with your article's window. How will you know when your pal Susan responds with juicy details about the party last night?

 If your sound is turned on, you'll hear the IM chime.

 If your sound is off or otherwise not available (read: broken), move the IM title bar to a visible spot (this may involve sizing your other window down a bit). When Susan's gossip appears on your IM screen at last, you'll see a close bracket (aka a

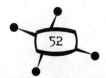

greater-than sign) on the title bar just before the Instant Message From line.

| 🔺 >Instant Message From: SusieFB | _ ☐ ✕ |

TIP

If you inadvertently cover your IM window with another, you don't have to frantically close windows until you find your correspondence. Just choose Window ➤ Instant Message From, and it'll come to the fore.

YOUR BUDDY LIST

Your Buddy List is the easiest way to tell whether a cherished friend is online and thus available for instant messaging. When one of your buddies logs on, her name will pop up in the Buddy List window. You can then seize the moment and send her an IM (or an invitation to a private chat room, where you two can converse freely). To set up your Buddy List group:

1. Select My AOL ➤ Buddy List.

2. Click the Create button.

3. In the Create a Buddy List Group dialog box, enter a group name (online buds, DOOM players, biking club, whatever).

4. One at a time, type each pal's screen name into the Enter a Screen Name box and click Add Buddy.

5. Click Save when you're done.

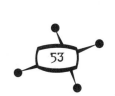

After you've gotten started with your Buddy List setup, everything else is self-explanatory. You can edit a group, create more groups (after you get addicted to Ultima Online, for

Member Directory

instance, you'll need to create a new group to keep track of your guild members). Notice you can refer to the Member Directory if you forget a friend's screen name (of course, this strategy only works if he has a Member Profile).

Buddy List™ Preferences

Click Buddy List Preferences to get to your Buddy List window preferences; here you can choose to automatically open your Buddy List when you sign onto AOL, and you can associate sounds with Buddy List occurrences (so you're notified when pals sign on and off).

Now that you've set up your list, the Buddy List window will show you which of your friends are online and, with the handy Locate button, let you locate them (so you can sneak up behind them in whatever chat room they're hanging out in and surprise them), easily send them instant messages, and invite them to a private chat room.

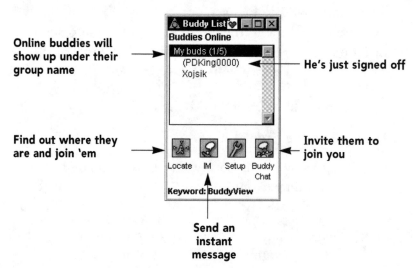

Online buddies will show up under their group name →

He's just signed off

Find out where they are and join 'em →

Invite them to join you

Send an instant message

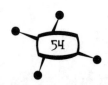

Buddy List Sounds Just for You

You can customize buddy list sounds; when a bud comes online you'll be notified by the sound file of your choice. First you need to install the default sounds, then you can play.

To install default buddy list sounds:

1. Open up your buddy list by choosing My AOL ➤ Buddy List.

2. Click the Buddy List Preferences button.

3. Choose when you wish to hear a sound (when a buddy signs on or when she signs off), then click the Go to Sound Library button.

4. Select Download Buddy Sound Installer "Door Theme," then click Download Now (or Later).

5. When you've downloaded the file, navigate to the directory it was downloaded to (usually C:\AOL 4.0\Download\ Buddoor.exe).

6. Double-click on buddoor.exe to install it.

Now customize your Buddy List sounds with these easy steps:

1. Download a cool buddyesque .WAV file to your hard drive (you can find more .WAV files in the Buddy List Sound Library or in AOL's shareware heap).

2. Follow the path: Start ➤ Settings ➤ Control Panel.

3. Double-click the Sound icon.

4. In the Sound Properties dialog box there are several Events sections; under the Windows section, click the Buddy In event.

5. Move to the Name box directly underneath the Events box and click the Browse button.

Continued

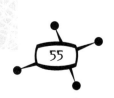

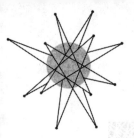

6. Navigate to the folder containing the perfect .WAV for your buddies to be ushered in by, select the file, and click OK.

7. Repeat for as many other sound files as you like.

8. When you're done, click OK.

9. Restart AOL for the new sounds to take effect.

NOTE

A newly online bud will show up with an asterisk next to her name (just so you can keep all those buds straight). A recently logged-off pal will be indicated by the parentheses enclosing his screen name.

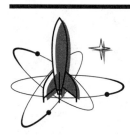

TIP

If you have a lot of buddy list categories (coworkers, gamers, high school friends, college friends, ex-coworkers, and so on), you can manage who shows up in your Buddy List by double-clicking the categories you don't care to see expanded. If it's the weekend, you may not care who of your coworkers is online; just double-click your co-workers category, and all you'll see is the category name with either a plus (+) sign or nothing next to it, depending on whether someone is logged on or not. The (+) sign indicates that the group is collapsed. The numbers after it, (0/5) or (1/5), tell you how many buddies from that group are signed on. (If you see from the parenthetical numbers that a coworker is online and succumb to curiosity, you can always double-click the category to see what hard worker is slaving away over the weekend.)

RECORDING IM TEXT

Say you want to keep your IM conversation for posterity (what *posterity* means to you I'll refrain from speculating on). Choose My Files ➤ Log Manager and enable Session Logs. Be sure to click the Log Instant Message Conversations box within the Session Logs section. And you're on! I get into the details of logging sessions in Chapter 3, *Wowing the Chat Room*.

ADDING STUFF

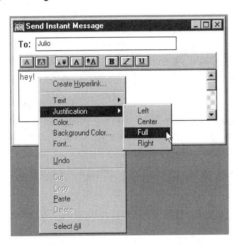

There's more to instant messaging than meets the eye. If you right-click on the text box, you'll find another layer of possibilities within easy reach. You can add a URL (if you have it memorized), play with the text justification, change the font of your message, and access the editing options already available in the IM toolbar.

Cool AOL sites and Web sites are simple to share via IM (yes, uncool sites are just as easy to share):

 To share a Favorite Place, open your Favorite Places list, select the Fave Place you wish to share, and drag it to the IM text box. Once dropped, it'll turn blue and underscore itself, becoming an automatic hyperlink for your IM recipient to follow and enjoy.

 To share a URL from an open Web window, just drag and drop the heart into your IM text box.

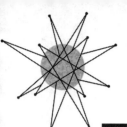

TIP

If you don't want the hyperlink to show up with the default text (such as an undescriptive URL), type something more enticing into the IM box, select the portion you want to become a hyperlink, and right-click. Choose Create Hyperlink, enter the URL (or copy it from the URL box and paste it here), and click OK.

PowerTools

PowerTools is a shareware program that replaces AOL's toolbar with its own, keeping AOL's functions and adding many more. PowerTools allows selective IM reception (upon receipt, PowerTools will automatically close IMs from AOLies you designate as scum but allow IMs from all the cool people), allows you to send and receive WAV files in IMs (but only with other PowerTools users), combines all your IM goings-on into one window for easier multi-IMing (you power IMer, you), automatically logs your IMs—and a whole lot more that has nothing to do with instant messages.

If you're online a lot and need a functionality boost (or just a new toy), PowerTools is worth checking out.

You can find the shareware program PowerTools at keyword: **bps**. Once there, click the Software Library button and choose your weapon. The 32-bit version of PowerTools closest to the top of the list (meaning more recent) is the one you're looking for. You can check it out for 20 days, after which you'll need to register it and pay a small fee for its continued use.

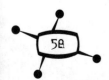

SECRET

In your perusal of the groovy new and improved message boards posted around AOL space (these are the ones with the pile-o'-pushpins background), you may have noticed that some people have creative signatures that perform tricks like bringing up a Write Mail window or IM window with their screen name already in place. Sound cool? Want to get IMs from message-board readers? Follow the steps under The Message Board Signature Secret in Chapter 1, but instead of typing **E-mail Me!** in the Place Description box and *mailto:YourScreenName@ aol.com* into the Internet Address box, type **IM me!** (or whatever you wish to say) in the Place Description box and **aol://9293:** *YourScreenName* (for instance, **aol://9293: LArendal**) in the Internet Address box.

WHAT TO DO ABOUT IM UNDESIRABLES

You're chatting innocently away, or even just flitting from room to room, when an instant message chimes up in the corner of your screen. You don't recognize the name, but from what you can gather from the message, you're about to be disconnected from AOL! To save your account from annihilation, you'll need to send your password to the IMer, who seems to be an AOL official.

As if you can't read the permanent message embedded in all IM windows: *AOL staff will never ask for your password or billing information.*

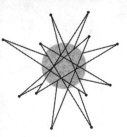

The above scenario happens more often than you'd expect; such password scammers get lists of people in chat rooms (and I show you how in Chapter 3; that part's perfectly legal), then IM each of them, hoping someone will fall for the ruse. Once they have your password, they can log on as you and do all sorts of dastardly things in your name. Well, we can't have that! There are a bunch of things you can do to protect yourself from IM evil:

 Turn all IMs off (you won't be able to send or accept any IMs).

 Selectively block specific screen names from IMing you (and conveniently blocking yourself from those screen names' Buddy Lists).

 Reply to the harassing IMer by sending a separate IM threatening to report him if he continues (and then report him).

 Minimize the IM window and go about your business while the harasser sends as many IMs as she pleases until her evil little fingers are worn into tiny nubbins.

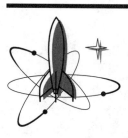

TIP

If you're on AOL 3 and you receive an IM that causes your system to freeze, record the IMer's name before you reboot and then, when you're back up, take the steps outlined in *Password Scammers* to report the violation. In the Paste a Copy of the Solicitation Here box, type the offender's name and **IM punt**. AOL staffers will understand what you're talking about—AOL 3 has a mostly harmless bug that fiendishly clever IM programming can manipulate to cause screen freeze. Consider upgrading.

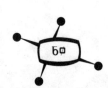

TURNING ALL INSTANT MESSAGES OFF (AND THEN ON AGAIN)

If you're too busy to chat or you just have a good, old-fashioned temper tantrum of the "Leave me alone! Just leave me alone!" variety, you can temporarily turn away all IMs to you. *Temporarily* here means until you're ready to receive them again.

To turn IM reception off:

1. Open up a fresh IM window (Ctrl+I).

2. In the To field, type **$im_off**.

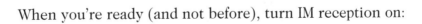

NOTE

The dollar sign tells the AOL computer that the sequence is a command, which sets it up to receive and implement the *im off* command.

3. In the message box, type something, anything. It can be one random character. But there has to be something there or the IM won't transmit.

4. Send the instant message (Ctrl+Enter or Tab+ Spacebar).

When you're ready (and not before), turn IM reception on:

1. Open up an IM window (Ctrl+I).

2. Type **$im_on**.

3. Again, enter something into the message box.

4. Send it (Ctrl+Enter or Tab+Spacebar).

And you're back in circulation.

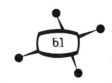

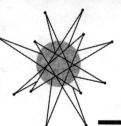

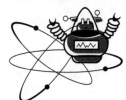

WARNING

Keep in mind that IMs are always automatically *on* when you sign on, regardless of how you left 'em in your previous AOL session.

SELECTIVELY BLOCKING IMS AND BUDDY LIST RECOGNITION

You really like Aunt Grace, but she does go on—and she's online all the time! Sometimes you just want to surf in peace. I feel for you, and I'm here to tell you, you can alter your Buddy List preferences to shield your presence from Aunt Grace's prying Buddy List eyes.

To block an AOLie's Buddy List from detecting your presence and her IMs from reaching you:

1. If your Buddy List isn't already jostling for attention on your screen, choose My AOL ➤ Buddy List.

2. Choose Privacy Preferences.

3. To block Aunt Grace, click the third radio button (see Figure 2.3)—Block Only Those People Whose Screen Names I List.

NOTE

Note that with radio buttons you can only operate within the choice you've made; you can't Block Aunt Grace *and* Allow Only LArendal, for instance.

4. Fill in her screen name in the right-hand field and click Add.

5. Choose between your privacy options at the bottom; either block her Buddy List but allow IMs (should she figure out you're online), or block both.

Privacy Preferences
Allows you to control who can see and contact you online

What is
AOL Instant
Messenger™?

Choose Your Privacy Preferences

○ Allow all AOL members and AOL Instant Messenger users
○ Block AOL Instant Messenger users only
◉ Block only those people whose screen names I list
○ Allow only those people whose screen names I list
○ Block all AOL members and AOL Instant Messenger users

Apply Preferences to the Following Features

○ Buddy List
◉ Buddy List and Instant Message

Type screen name here:

[   ] Add

auntgrace

Remove

Save   Cancel   Help

FIGURE 2.3: Don't call me, I'll call *you*.

NOTE

Blocking someone with Buddy List privacy preferences will disable his Buddy List recognition of you and also disallow him from using Locate or the Available button in the IM window to find you. However, if you have a Member Profile and your blockee checks it out, a red arrow will point to your name when you're online.

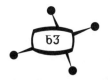

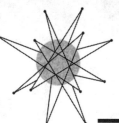

WARNING

Keep in mind that if you block someone from IMing you, you won't be able to IM her either. Either *both* of you can IM, or *neither* of can.

REPORTING IM HARASSERS WHILE CONSERVING CLICKS

As I outlined in *Password Scammers*, you should definitely report IM abusers. If you get sick of clicking through all those windows time after time, try these remedies:

 Add the Notify AOL screen (at keyword: **TOS** ➤ Report a Violation button) to your Favorite Places list by dragging and dropping the heart icon onto the Favorites folder (or just pressing Ctrl++). When it comes time to report that special someone, just choose Favorites ➤ Keyword: Notify AOL.

 Better yet, create a shortcut so you can hit a two-key keyboard combination and be right where you wanna be.

To create a shortcut to the TOS violations window, recreate the following steps:

1. Choose Favorites ➤ My Shortcuts ➤ Edit Shortcuts.

2. In the resulting Edit Shortcut Keys window, shown in Figure 2.4, add **TOS Violation** to a column on the left (either an empty slot or one you want to replace) and **notifyaol** to the right slot opposite.

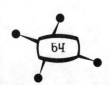

Shortcut Title	Keyword/Internet Address	Key
Discover America Online|	discover	Ctrl + 1
What's Hot	hot	Ctrl + 2
Top News	top news	Ctrl + 3
AOL Live	events	Ctrl + 4
Stock Quotes	stocks	Ctrl + 5
Sign on a Friend	friend	Ctrl + 6
AOL Store	aolstore	Ctrl + 7
TOS Violation	notifyaol	Ctrl + 8
		Ctrl + 9
		Ctrl + 0

Save Changes Cancel Help

What it is **Where it is** **How to get there**

FIGURE 2.4: Shortcut your way to the top.

3. Click Save Changes.

Now whenever you want to report a violation, you can copy the violating text and hit the keyboard shortcut (Ctrl+8 in my example) to go directly to the Notify AOL window. If you hate remembering keyboard shortcuts, you can instead choose Favorites ➤ My Shortcuts ➤ TOS Violation.

NOTE

Of course, you can use these 10 reserved shortcut keys for anything you want—and you can certainly override AOL's default shortcuts.

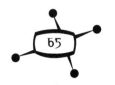

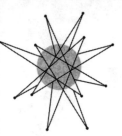

JUST IGNORE 'EM

To ignore a stream of instant messages from one person, just minimize the IM window (click the title bar button with the underscore).

Minimize—make tiny—ignore

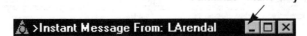

She can send you as many IMs as she likes; they'll all go into that tiny little box you've shoved into a dark corner on your screen. Because each person gets his own instant message window, you can still send and receive instant messages to and from friends without a problem.

When you've finished surfing and chatting with socially adept AOL members, open the IM window, copy the message (you don't have to scroll through and read it; just choose Edit ➤ Select All, then Edit ➤ Copy), and report the creep as detailed in *What to Do about IM Undesirables*.

IMs OF THE FUTURE

Instant gratification is a higher good in our society. It helps the economy by keeping cash—used to indulge our every whim—flowing, it gives us that little desire-and-acquire rush (kind of a Prozac for capitalists), and the intrinsic nature of instantaneous purchasing leaves enough room in the day for a little quality time with the family. Instant gratification is unquestionably American; life, liberty, and the pursuit of happiness right here, ladies and gentlemen. Step right up.

Instant messaging is a part of this way of life; it is moving irrevocably toward instant access of everything to everyone; phone

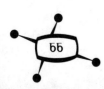

capabilities, spontaneous art, video capabilities (don't forget to take out those curlers!), paging…. You can already access AOL from your TV's cable modem. The next iteration of AOL will surely be installable on your cell phone for complete portability and availability.

MY BONNY LIES OVER THE INTERNET: IMING WITH NON-AOLIES

Instant messages, once little goldfish swimming in a little pool, have burst past the floodgate and are now braving the ocean waters of the Internet. Luckily, AOL's Instant Messenger makes those stormy seas fairly benign.

WARNING

You must be 18 or older to use Instant Messenger. Also, by the time you read this, AIM will most likely not be free.

To converse via AIM with a non-AOL friend:

1. Have your friend sign up for AOL's Instant Messenger, available for download from AOL's home page at http://www.aol.com. He will need to pick an AOL-type screen name and tell you what it is.

2. Add his screen name to your Buddy List.

3. Make sure he has your e-mail address (ScreenName@ aol.com—for instance, LArendal@aol.com) on his Buddy List.

4. Proceed as normal; his address will appear in your Buddy List when he's online (using his Web browser) and vice

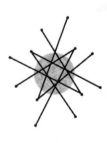

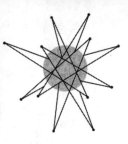
versa. If he's online, just select his name and click IM to bring up an IM window with his address already in the To box.

When your AOL Instant Messenger buddy IMs you, you'll get a knock-knock window like that in Figure 2.5.

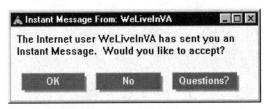

FIGURE 2.5: Cheaper than a collect call, AIM clearly identifies who's knocking on your AOL screen.

PAGING

Paging. Everyone does it—doctors, teenagers, drug dealers. And now you can add even more people to the always-available fray of pagees rushing to pay phones or striding down the street talking into their little plastic boxes.

Here's how:

1. Choose People ➤ Send Message to Pager.

2. Set your pagee of choice up in your pager's Address Book by clicking the Address Book button and then choosing Create.

3. Type in your pagee's name (16 characters maximum).

4. Enter the pager ID in the appropriate field.

5. For well-rounded access, you can send a copy of each page to your pagee's e-mail address. If you'd like to do so, enable that option and enter her e-mail address.

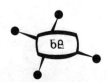

N⊕TE

This name doesn't have to be your friend's real name or full name; it just needs to be recognizable to you and unique from all your other pagee entries.

Once the Address Book entry has been successfully completed, it will close automatically. Now that your friend's pager ID has been recorded, all you have to do is select her entry from your Paging Address Book, and it will be placed in the Send a Page ID Number box. Then just type in your message and press Send.

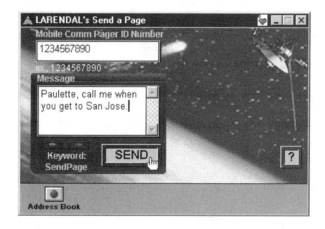

N⊕TE

Send a Page only works with digital pagers, and currently only digital pagers from AT&T and Mobile Comm. In addition, the pager must support alphanumeric paging to successfully receive your page.

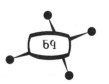

Chapter 3

Wowing the Chat Room

AOL is the perfect place to meet people online. For one thing, there are a lot of people there to meet, and most of them want to meet you. For another, you can flit about from room to room all night without entering the same room twice. And you can assume whatever persona you want for the evening's entertainment. If you're shy, you can lurk and listen. If you're outgoing, you can entertain the room.

Of course, there are drawbacks. There's the lowest-common-denominator factor, where the most asinine person sets the conversational tone. And, unfortunately, there seem to be a fair number of lowest common denominators in chat rooms. There's also the isolation thing; as much as you can successfully connect with people over the net, you're still just sitting in front of a computer screen in the end. And who knows if those you connect to are really who they say they are? Meeting people online adds a whole new level of anxiety to interpersonal relationships.

However, it's still possible to find kindred spirits hanging out, willing to engage in intelligent discourse. Let's go find them!

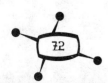

WHICH WAY TO THE CHAT ROOM?

People Connection, the easiest and biggest floodgate to chatting, is accessible right from the Welcome window as well as from the toolbar (People ➤ People Connection). If you've used People ➤ Locate AOL Member Online to find a friend online and she's in a chat room, you can join her with the click of a button.

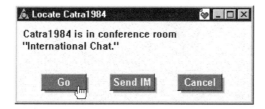

NOTE

Chat rooms and conference rooms are pretty much the same thing. Chat rooms are mostly accessed from People Connection, conference rooms from the different areas around AOL. Chat rooms are usually more unruly, and they hold 23 people max (more if there are AOL guides present). Conference rooms can hold 48 people, and the discussions are for the most part on topic. Auditoriums, where special live events take place, have virtually unlimited seating (but everyone's placed in rows, so the chatting doesn't get too overwhelming).

It's not hard to find people chatting away, but how do you find people chatting about what *you* want to chat about?

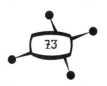

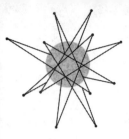
FROM PEOPLE CONNECTION

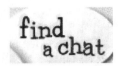

Once you get to the People Connection area on AOL (shown in Figure 3.1), you have some choices in front of you. Click Find a Chat to get the listing of featured chats shown in Figure 3.2.

FIGURE 3.1: Take off your coat and hat and dive in to find the real action.

Featured Chats

In the featured chats—which are AOL-created and monitored—you can check out the chat rooms by double-clicking a category in the left box, then double-clicking a room in the right box, as I've done in Figure 3.2.

Some tips:

Town Square is pretty generic; you'd best be prepared to be the life of the party or be bored.

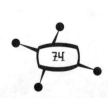

 Special Interest rooms bear very specific names that allow you to pick your room wisely. Many people in these rooms actually chat intelligently, with complete sentences and without expletives, about the subject at hand.

 Click the Who's Chatting button to check the list before you enter (and thus avoid or find certain people).

 If the More button is active, click it to expand the list.

 If you've forgotten when the Tamagotchi virtual pet chat is scheduled, click the Featured Chats Schedule button to browse through AOL's scheduled chat selection or search the feature chats (with the Search Featured Chats button) using AND, OR, and NOT to link key concepts. (See Chapter 5 for a thorough discussion of boolean expressions.)

Member Chats

In the member chats, you'll find the same sorts of categories as in the featured chats (as you see in Figure 3.3), but the chat rooms themselves are member-created.

 Town Square and Special Interests are usually full of all sorts of nasty rooms (in both good and bad senses of the word).

 You *can* find some interesting stuff going on in some of the more specific categories, like people guessing a song from the lyrics (yeah, some of these are nasty, too), people discussing abortion

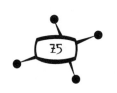

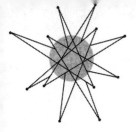

(in between the usual banter), and people hotly debating the merits of certain sports teams. However, most of the rooms here will promise much and deliver little—unless you just wanna goof around for a couple of hours.

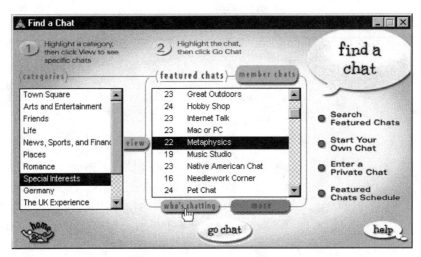

FIGURE 3.2: I'm about to check out who's getting metaphysical at this late hour...

You can also create your own room in any Member Chat category by clicking Start Your Own Chat ➤ Member Chat. Give it a catchy title that'll draw people in (but not too catchy or you'll draw the wrong people, if you know what I mean and I think you do).

Click the Search Member Chats button to find that special room. Unfortunately, you'll only be able to search for the exact title of the room, so you'll be doing a lot of mindreading to find a room on a specific topic (would it be Jersey Artists or New Jersey Artists or NJ Artists or...).

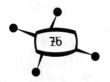

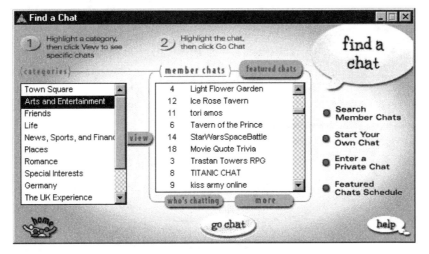

FIGURE 3.3: Member chat. Yawn.

Private Chat

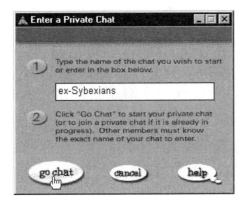

The private chat rooms are, well, private. They're also extremely useful for conversations with more than two other people. Say, for instance, two of your ex-coworkers—now living in Texas and Massachusetts, while you've stayed in California—are online and you all want to talk. By clicking on the Enter a Private Chat button, you can create a private chat room and IM them the name (see Chapter 2 for tips on Instant Messaging), thus inviting them in. Despite the multiple threads of conversation that inevitably get tangled during online chat, it's a great way to hang out with old friends.

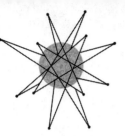

Buddy Chat

The easiest way to create a private room and invite your friends in is to have them in your buddy list. When they're online, gather them to your online party by highlighting the screen names you want to invite in the Buddy List window and clicking the Buddy Chat button.

SECRET

You can also get into private chat rooms by guessing at names. There are certain private rooms that always exist that you can slip into without drawing too much attention to yourself, because they're often full. Given the nature of many of the member chat rooms, you'll most likely be able to guess at the names of these private rooms.

OTHER CHAT CHANNELS

From Channel Chat (keyword **channel chat**) you can connect to conference rooms all over AOL, get into game rooms, look for that special someone…. The chat opportunities from Channel Chat can be superb.

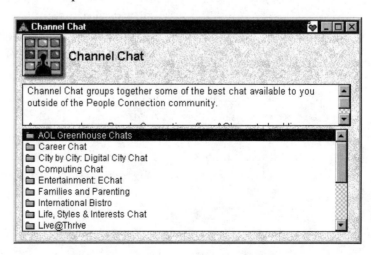

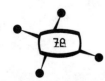

Also try your chat-room-surfing luck at AOL Live! (keyword **aol live**). Get into the Today's Live Events listing and scroll through the list of chat rooms on the bottom left; here you'll find the chat rooms associated with AOL's Channels area.

Meeting and Greeting

It's Thursday evening, you're bored, you're wishing you had someone across the world to visit so you could take a vacation from the dreariness at home, when you realize you *could* meet someone across the world—and then go visit them. And it's almost easier done than said!

Here are the best meeting spots on AOL:

Digital city: keyword **Talk of the Town**. Here you can connect with AOL members in your city or another, look for jobs, and find out what's shakin'.

Romance Channel: keyword **Romance**. What it sounds like!

Love@AOL: It's its own keyword, and it's a fave among AOLies seeking that luv-induced endorphin high.

Member Directory: People ➤ Search AOL Member Directory. Search through the Member Directory for people claiming similar interests to yours. Use the Advanced Search tab to get way specific (more about this in *Search the Member Directory*).

Chat rooms: Search for chats on subjects that interest you; if the room members are really discussing the stated topic, you may meet some interesting folk. From chat rooms you can strike up an IM conversation or send e-mail.

Continued

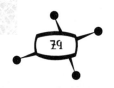

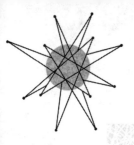

Conference rooms: The same idea as chat rooms, but found outside of People Connection and thus containing conversations usually relevant to their intended topics. Start from Channel Chat (keyword **channel chat**) and AOL Live! (keyword **aol live**), but also explore your favorite AOL areas to see if they have chat rooms.

Newsgroups: keyword **newsgroups**. Check out others' opinions on a topic that interests you (e.g., world peace, fencing, doll collections) in a message-board-like forum. Strike up e-mail conversations with newsgroup members you're intrigued by.

Pen pals: keyword **Special Delivery**. Sign up to receive and/or send e-mail to other people looking for new correspondents.

Mailing lists: keyword **mailing list**. Sign up for a slew of e-mail on a topic you're similarly obsessed with. Send friendly e-mail to those who pique your curiosity.

Message boards (yes, even message boards): Opportunities to connect exist everywhere. Check out the message boards you'll find in areas all over AOL; you'll learn interesting tidbits—and you'll find people whose signatures include invitations to e-mail or IM them.

Stuff You Oughta Know

Okay, now that you've been introduced to the AOL network of chat-sters, you'll want to refine your style. Here are some tips.

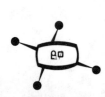

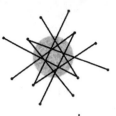

CHATTQUETTE

Don't swear. It's not very interesting conversation (and frankly, it makes you look really @#$%ing dumb).

Don't SCREAM. It's offensive.

Don't be a jerk. You'll get a rep, and you could get kicked off.

Type the first 3 or 4 letters of the screen name you're responding to when you type a response. This tactic is especially helpful if there's a bunch of people in the room and many conversations going at once.

Catra1984:   MEstu: I agree. But it's been too long, I think, to change it.

If people greet you

Hi Catra!

or wave at you

::waving at Catra::

respond in kind.

PROTECT YOUR RIGHT TO QUALITY CHAT

You can dismiss idiots from your otherwise-pleasant experience: Double-click on the name of the rude chatter and, in the Information About dialog box that comes up, check the Ignore Member button. Once a chatter is Ignored, his comments won't show up on your scrolling chat screen anymore.

Click here to erase Catra's nonsense from view

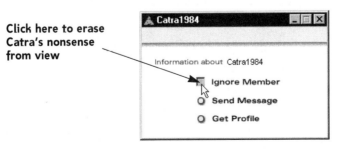

103

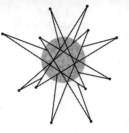

If you're experiencing continuing harassment—you've Ignored him, turned off your IMs, but he's sent you a flood of e-mail—report his butt to the Terms of Service (TOS) people. If you have evidence of TOS violations in chat or IM, type keyword **TOS** into the Go box and click Report a Violation in the Terms of Service window. If you have offensive e-mail, forward it to **TOSemail1** (and then go block him from e-mail as I discuss in Chapter 2).

NOTE

I discuss violations and how to report them with ease in Chapter 2, *IMing with Ease and Sophistication*.

CHAT PREFERENCES

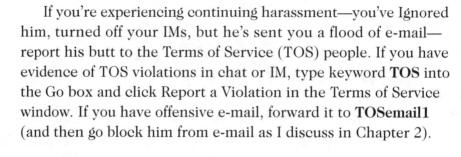

Chat

Now that you have some chat experience, you'll want to customize some of the more perfunctory chat options. From the toolbar, choose My AOL ➤ Preferences and click the Chat button.

Here you can decide how you want to experience the chat room. You can keep tabs on who's coming and going, you can alphabetize for a neater, more precise experience, you can double-space the lines you see to make who said what clearer (it makes the screen scroll twice as fast, though), and you can decide whether to hear or tune out sounds.

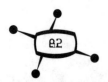

MEMBER DIRECTORY

Another way you can go about chatting is to search the Member Directory for people who share your enthusiasm for chess, went to your alma mater, live in the town you grew up in, whatever. To get to the Member Directory, choose People ➤ Search AOL Member Directory.

As you can see in Figure 3.4, you have some options for narrowing down your search. You can type location-specific and name-specific search words into the appropriate fields, or type keywords into the search-everything field.

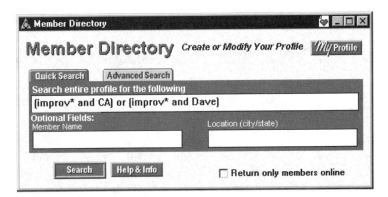

FIGURE 3.4: If you ever meet a guy at a party and wonder whether he's on AOL, this would be a way to find out—short of actually asking him.

The Advance Search tab offers you the option of filling in everything about the person you seek. If you knew this much about a person, you'd know her screen name, don't you think?? Seriously, though, if you're looking for other Mac users, this is a great way to search for people with whom you can share resources. The Advance Search tab can be incredibly useful if the person you're looking for uses AOL's Member Profile fields in the manner intended—which will not always be the case.

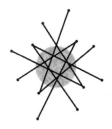

Get Specific with Booleans

Boolean expressions, sprinkled liberally throughout Figure 3.4, link search criteria in a sort of shorthand. Wildcards substitute for blanks that could be anything. To use them, follow these easy rules:

*	substitutes for any string of characters	**hand*** will result in handsome, handy, handful, etc.
?	substitutes for one letter	**wom?n** will result in woman, women, womyn, womon, and so on
and	search will reveal only profiles containing both words	**cat and dog** will result in people who mention both animals in their profile
or	search will reveal profiles with either word	**Sinhalese or Sri Lanka** will result in people who mention either in their profile
( )	group words together so you can search for a couple of different options at a time	**(improv and CA) or (improv and Dave)** will result in CA residents and Daves who profess an interest in improv; the Daves will not necessarily be CA residents, the CA residents not necessarily named Dave.

Augmenting Chat

There are several ways to extend and enhance your chat experience on the fly:

Instant Message   If you find someone you click with, you can always take your conversation "off-chat" by sending him an IM; from there you can chat in peace, without

having to sift through the other 21 threads scrolling down your screen. Double-click on his screen name in the chat room's People Here box and click the Send Message button in the Information About dialog box.

Member Profile   You can check out anyone's profile by double-clicking their screen name and, in the super-useful Information About dialog box, clicking the Get Profile button. This action pops up the Member Profile belonging to the object of your scrutiny; if you're interested in inquiring further into her hobbies, by all means ask.

Ignore Member   As I discuss in several other places in this chapter, the Ignore Member button is a boon to us rational

☐ **Ignore Member**

folk who don't like to be subjected to multi-line spews nor be subjected to screaming (and nonscreaming) morons. Again, double-click the screen name in the People Here box and enable the Ignore Member box. Blessed relief follows.

WARNING

An ignored spewer often feels slighted by the lack of response and will do anything to get your attention back. Unfortunately, it's rather easy; all she has to do is leave the room and re-enter, and the Ignore you put on her will reset.

Notify AOL   If you're so offended by someone's behavior in a chat room that you feel Ignoring is too good for him, the handy Notify AOL button will allow you to record the lines in question for the Community Action Team to handle. Hate chat always falls into this category if you ask me.

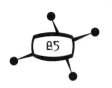

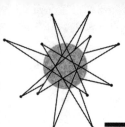

NOTE

Lest you think me contemptuous of the chat experience, let me say: I'm only contemptuous of the AOL members who ruin other people's legitimate conversations, whether by rude behavior, vulgarity, or plain mean-spiritedness (like harassment).

PowerTools

As I discussed in Chapter 2, *Instant Messaging with Ease and Sophistication*, PowerTools software is a real help in AOL. Found at keyword **bps**, PowerTools has some chat-specific capabilities you'll want to explore. These include the Get In! feature, which gets you into the chat room you want to be in; chat fonts and colors, which allows you to change the font size of your chat without having to reset your whole screen appearance; inactive chat list, which allows you to ignore that special someone even if she leaps out of the room and back in; and macro capabilities, so you can create multi-line characters of your own. To use sparingly, of course.

YOUR LOOK: CHATTING IN STYLE

With the new and improved chat room options, you can have even more fun with your words and pictures (I discuss ways to find picture ideas under *Conversational Spice*). The chat toolbar

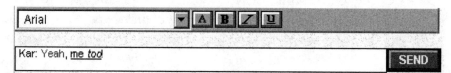

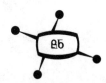

allows you to change fonts, color your letters, and to bold, italicize, and underline them. That's a lot of stuff to do to one little line of text!

The best use of color occurs with the doodads you can send. One of my favorites is a rose:

@>—->——

If you color the @ red, the >> brown, and the —— green, you've got a sweet picture to send someone.

Just a note about the font change; the text in chat rooms is so small that, unless people have set their displays to show large

Hey, that's just not nice! fonts, many of the fancy fonts will look like tiny pieces of tangled yarn.

To remedy the unreadable-yarn effect, you can make the font larger, of course, but keep in mind that yarn at any size isn't easy to read, and other room members might get annoyed with you.

NOTE

If you find that chat room fonts are too small to read, you can change your system fonts by right-clicking on your desktop and choosing Properties ➤ Settings and, in the Font Size box, choosing Large Fonts. If this option is unavailable to you, choose the Appearance tab and, in the Scheme box, select any of the large options.

Other ways to have fun with your words are to use shorthands and doodads.

CONVERSATIONAL SPICE

Typing is a lot of effort. Some of us do it well, some struggle through with two fingers and a lot of grief—not to mention spelling mistakes. There are shortcuts you can take to

communicate emotions and ideas without having to explain yourself in eloquent phrases.

Shorthands

Acronyms like LOL (laughing out loud), BTW (by the way), or AFK (away from keyboard) are commonly used in chat rooms. You can find a list of other common shorthands at keyword **shorthand**. You can also make up your own. If you see an acronym you just don't get, don't be shy about asking its utterer what it means.

Not really shorthand, but very useful, are colons and brackets. Colons are often used around actions, as if the stage directions from a play are being read:

:::walks to the door laughing:::

Brackets to signal hugs:

{{{{Catra}}}}

Doodads

Even more fun than shorthands are the little pictures people draw with Qwerty the keyboard. Doodads are emoticons' next generation; they express ideas through pictures, rather than mimicking facial expressions. For instance, rather than sending a sweetie a stick-figure kissy face, type a picture of a valentine heart. Like your writing teachers always said (and still say): show, don't tell. Doodads do just that. (Though, like emoticons, you never quite know what direction your head's supposed to be tilting; just think of it as good stretching exercise for the neck.)

<3	heart
>^..^<	cat
<^.,.^>	another cat
o/	raised hand

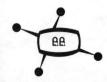

FRENCH SMILEYS

You all know about emoticons, so I won't rehash the oldies but goodies. However, there are a lot of emotiartists out there; to find some inventive smileys, go to keyword **smiley** to find French smileys.

Some of my favorites:

%\v	Picasso
:D	big laugh
> ><}}}^>	fish
@>—->——	rose
~=	a candle (message is a flame)

CDN SMILEYS

Go to keyword **CDN Smileys** to get the Canadian take on smileys. For instance:

(8-)	a hooting owl
@@@@@:-)	Marge Simpson (especially if the @'s are blue!)

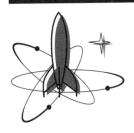

TIP

The smiley resources available to you, my virtual emoter, are, like everything on the Internet and (to a lesser extent) AOL, in flux. To find more smileys, I recommend doing a search for *smileys* or *emoticons* through Find ➤ Find It on AOL.

SOUND FILES

If your soundcard exists and is working, you'll be able to hear chat room sounds—and send them!

SENDING WAV FILES

Send a sound to the entire room by typing {S *filename*. (The capital S is very important; {s won't work.) Keep in mind that you're not actually *sending* a sound file, you're reaching into another person's computer (specifically, into their C:\America Online 4.0 directory) and activating its sound file. In other words, others in the room will only be able to hear the sound files that they have installed on their computers. If you send a sound that a chatter doesn't have installed, she won't hear a thing. So if you type

> **{S welcome**

the chat room members whose speakers are on and sound cards are working will hear Mr. AOL say "Welcome!" as is his wont (AOL comes with Welcome.wav, so everyone has it). However, if you type

> **{S leaving**

only those with Leaving.wav will hear a vampire cackle merrily about leaving Windows.

If you want to combine a sentence with a sound, bracket the command and filename like so:

> **{S welcome}**

You might say, for instance:

> **Catra! {S welcome} hello! Long time no chat!**

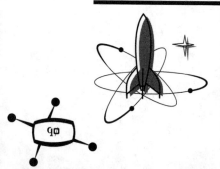

TIP

If you accidentally land in a noisy room that you want to stay in, but you find your hangover is making you rather testy in the face of all those WAV files bouncing around, you can turn off your speakers. Or you can go to Chat Preferences, as discussed earlier in this chapter, and turn off chat room sounds until the ibuprofen kicks in.

FINDING WAV FILES

To download cool WAV files, from the AOL toolbar, click Find ➤ Software ➤ Shareware ➤ Music & Sound and type **event sounds** into the Keywords box. You'll find some WAV utilities (which

List More Files

may be useful if you want to create your own WAV files), and a lot of event sounds. You'll have to hit the List More Files button a number of times to see them all.

Download Now

Download Later

To download a file, highlight the one you want and just click the Download Now or Download Later button.

If you choose to delay your WAV file gratification and download the file later, you'll need to retrieve it

Download

from your Download Manager (when you're ready, of course). To do so, choose My Files ➤ Download Manager, highlight the file (or files) you wish to put on your hard drive, and click Download.

Once the WAV file is downloaded, move it into the main America Online 4.0 (or aol30) folder (C:\America Online 4.0 or C:\aol30, unless you changed this pathway when you installed AOL). Only then is it accessible to your chatting efforts.

SECRET

La Pub, your Buddy List, and People Connection have their own sound libraries. Download 'em all for an ear-splittingly good time!

WAVMAN

Find WavMan in AOL's software library by clicking Find ➤ Software ➤ Shareware ➤ Application (enter **WAVMan** into the Keyword box) ➤ WAVMAN32: V7.2 Chat Room Manager. You can

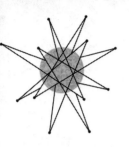

test drive it for 30 days, after which you'll need to register it and pay a small fee for its continued use.

Not only will WavMan give you hours of fiddling fun with your WAV files, it'll also let you create an automatic answer for IMs, create aliases for your commonly used screen names (so you can type in **Bente**—or just **B**—rather than **BIngesdtr**), create

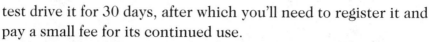 some cool-looking waves (strings of undulating char-acters), and, most exciting of all, enable the anti-logoff feature.

YOUR PROFILE

Once you enter a chat room, you are subject to scrutiny. Twenty-two other people immediately double-click your name and check out your Member Profile from the Information About dialog box.

Depending on what kind of attention you want to attract, you'll want to have a Member Profile. You could be sincere, silly, sarcastic, sensual…again, depending on what kind of attention you want coming your way.

To create a profile, choose My AOL ➤ My Member Profile and fill out whatever of the preset fields you want to fill out in the Edit Your Online Profile window shown in Figure 3.5. The first option, Your Name, will appear whether or not you fill it out, so you may as well fill it out so it doesn't look like you weren't paying attention. Otherwise you can ignore and embellish all you like.

THE SECRET to an ULtra—CooL ProFiLE

I can't believe anyone online really cares what kind of computer you're using (and if they do, they'll ask), and how many of us have a personal quote that sums up everything about us? I mean, really.

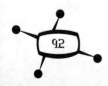

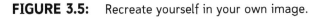

Edit Your Online Profile

To edit your profile, modify the category you would like to change and select
"Update." To continue without making any changes to your profile, select "Cancel."

Your Name:	
City, State, Country:	
Birthday:	
Sex:	○ Male ○ Female ⦿ No Response
Marital Status:	
Hobbies:	
Computers Used:	
Occupation:	
Personal Quote:	

Update   Delete   Cancel   My AOL   Help & Info

FIGURE 3.5:   Recreate yourself in your own image.

To ditch AOL's idea of interesting personal information and create fields that actually have something to do with you (or have nothing to do with anything), follow these steps:

1. Type in what you want others to think is your name. (It's okay if you want others to think your real name is your real name. Not everyone is as cynical as I am.)

WARNING

It's safest to only use your first name online at all times, including in your Member Profile.

2. Leaving the insertion point at the end of your "name" (nudge, nudge), press Ctrl+Backspace. A square will appear in the line; this square will translate into a new line in your Member Profile.

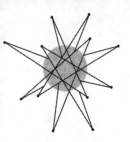

3. Type your unique new category—such as **Favorite Bands**—followed by a colon.

4. Press the Spacebar until you've covered about 30-38 spaces total, from beginning of your new line to end, and type in your descriptive text.

5. Repeat from step 2 until you run out of space (at which point your computer will beep in consternation, and you won't be able to type anything more on that line). Your profile will look something like the one in Figure 3.6.

TIP

If you want to cram a lot of information in, don't try to line up the descriptions. The spaces you use to line things up will detract from the amount of text you can enter.

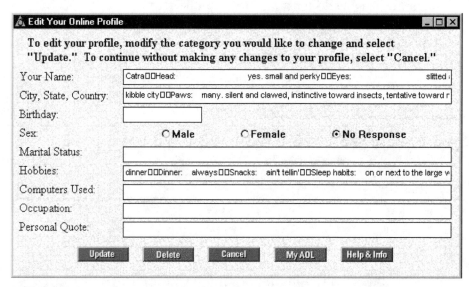

FIGURE 3.6:   Ever wonder what your cat is up to while you're at work?

Your Look: Chatting in Style

When you're satisfied with your sincerity, sarcasm, creative nonsense, or whatever you've put together, click Update. To see yourself as others see you (whew, that's a concept!), choose People ➤ Get AOL Member Profile (Ctrl+G). In the ensuing box, type in your screen name and click OK.

You'll be treated to a complete view of your statement of self, probably nothing like that of my alter-ego, Catra, as seen in Figure 3.7. Notice that I lined up the first few categories, which allowed only two extra fields before another canned field, Location, popped up. When I decided neat lines weren't for me, I got as many as five "information"-filled lines in between AOL-dictated categories (Location and Hobbies). I completely ignored Marital Status (n/a for a cat, you know) and many of the others; hence, they didn't show up.

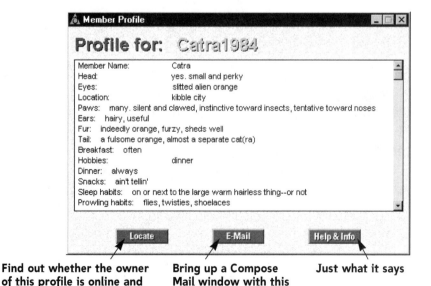

Find out whether the owner of this profile is online and in a chat room

Bring up a Compose Mail window with this screen name entered

Just what it says

FIGURE 3.7: Cats—on AOL?

95

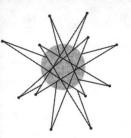

The advantages to the creative-writing approach are: It'll be a fun read for some, you may get some appreciative IMs, and you won't be as easy a target as if you'd written Female, Single (for instance). The disadvantage to such silliness is that if you are interested in hooking up with others in your area who enjoy going to live basketball games, this sort of Member Profile could not be considered effective advertising.

NOTE

Of course, it's *your* Member Profile, and you can change it as often as you wish. Once you've found all the basketball-game-going pals you need, you can turn yourself into the cat you always wanted to be by revamping your Member Profile.

COOL AND UNUSUAL CHAT

As you'll sense as you glance through the gems I've pulled out for you below, the best chat (read: interesting, fun, intellectually stimulating) with people you don't know can be found through Channel Chat, AOL Live!, and through your favorite online forums. Here you get away from the hordes of goofs who're just looking to recreate Beavis and Butthead in their own image(s).

Of course, everything depends on who's where. Even though these sites are well away from the madding crowd, once in a while one of them gets loose and mucks up a polite conversation about Paris' Picasso museum. This is where the Ignore Member button comes in handy, as discussed earlier under *Chatiquette*.

You'll also notice that these channel chat rooms (conference rooms, really) allow a whole lot more than 23 people in at a

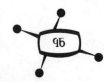

time: 48 is the max here. Clear communication—for instance, typing in the screen name of the chatter you're responding to as well as your response—becomes important in crowds such as these.

HECKLERS ONLINE

Hecklers Online is outrageous and intelligent. Not only do they allow—heck, *encourage*—a certain amount of abuse in their chat rooms, if you pick the right night, your HO (Hecklers Online) hosts may tolerate a certain amount of profanity. (In the name of fun and good heckling, of course.)

The best part about Hecklers Online is that they're creative. It's no fun just trashing other AOLies, so you can pick from word games (rewrite a Bible verse, heckler style), graffiti art (take Al Gore into your favorite paint program for a makeover—then post it on HO!), interactive jokes, and more. Take Absurd IMs, for example. In the last chapter I told you how to report the lame-brains who IM you for your password; Hecklers Online encourages you to play with them like a cat with a furry catnip toy. Check out keyword **HO** ➤ Funny Bone ➤ Absurd IMs to enjoy others' shenanigans and submit your own.

Heckler's Online introduction ──➤

Snert ──────────➤

The cat baiting the mouse ──➤

The mouse scurries away... ──➤

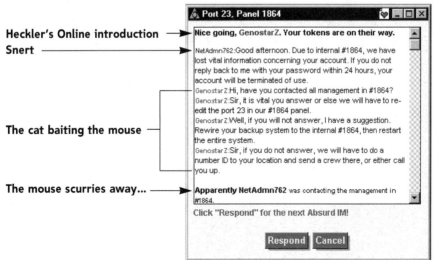

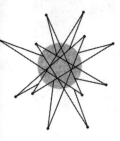

International Bistro

Keyword **bistro** will give you a chance to practice that high school French, or learn Tagalog, or just mingle with other citizens of the world.

The Front Porch

Even if you're not at all religious or spiritual, the Front Porch is pretty cool; it's an interfaith meeting ground for open-minded people to discuss ethics and their beliefs, and there is a weekly schedule of events that involves many faiths and philosophies. Like the other rooms I deem cool, the idiot factor is quite low here. Access the Front Porch through Channel Chat (keyword **channel chat**) ➤ Religion & Beliefs Chat ➤ Religion & Ethics Front Porch.

Cecil Adams' Chat

At keyword **Straight Dope** you can find Cecil Adams' straight answers to the goofiest questions. In addition, you can chat about said goofy questions.

Digital City Chat

At keyword **Talk of the Town** you'll get a plethora of chat choices. Sign up for chat with those in (or interested in) the city nearest you—or for chatting with residents of a city you want to go to. Once you select your city, you can select from a list of chat topics and times, or you can select your age group—from blastin' teens to golden gaters—from the list of free-for-all chat.

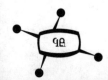

CHAT SCHEDULES

You can find some excellent chat, a la AOL Live!, at chat events with special guests. Just find areas that appeal to your tastes and check their guest schedule (usually posted prominently in the area) regularly (you'll find most of the rooms that feature special guests at AOL Live). In some areas you can sign up to get the chat schedules e-mailed to you.

EXPANDING YOUR OPPORTUNITES FOR MEANINGFUL CHAT

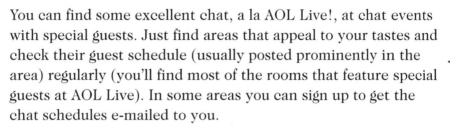

There are a lot of people yakkin' it up on AOL; about 9 million at last count. But that's only a subset of online chatters as a whole. Countless chat rooms exist all over the Internet, some of them quite creative. If you want to find regular scrollable-text chat out there on the Internet, get online and search for it . If you're ready for something more exotic, check out the venues listed below.

AVATAR CHAT

Avatar chat is cool and clunky. In avatar chat, you choose an avatar—which is a 2-D or 3-D rendering of something (usually a humanoid)—to represent you, and you float through chat rooms talking to other avatars. Depending on where you decide to chat avatar-style, you may be able to pick from fictional likenesses, fantastical space-age humanoids, comic-style drawings, animals, you name it. In many chat areas, you can use an image you've created with special avatar-creation software. Some avatar chat incorporates voice, so if you have a microphone, you can represent yourself vocally.

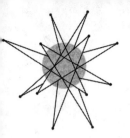

The downside to avatar chat is that each world requires you to own its third-party software to use it. Sometimes this software is free, often it is not. Therefore you are under a bit of pressure to make sure you choose your avatar world wisely, lest you waste $30 or so. Each avatar area will have links to sites where you can buy the software, so at least they make it easy for you to fork over for the goods. Also, each avatar world is negotiated in a different way; sometimes avatars are easy to manipulate, and sometimes you'll bang your head against the wall for a long time—literally. Coordination definitely helps.

Where to Find It

To find a list of avatar chats on the Internet, type **http://www.ccon.org/** into the Keyword/URL box and press Go. You'll find that The Contact Consortium has links to all kinds of avatar-type chats.

NOTE

Clnet reviewed several avatar chats on different platforms (Compuserve, MSN, etc.), and gave Worlds Chat the highest score. Check out the review at http://www.cnet.com/Content/Reviews/Compare/Chat/ss05d.html. Of course you have to buy Worlds' software to join in, but you can demo it free first at http://www.worlds.net.

Try Comic Chat at http://www.digital—space.com/avatars/cchat.html for a list of comic chats. Figure 3.8 shows an example of Microsoft's Comic Chat at play.

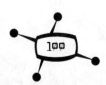

FIGURE 3.8: Catra's having a tough day.

For some more hot links to Virtual Worlds and the People Who Love Them, go to `http://www.ccon.org/hotlinks/hotlinks.html`. Here you'll be able to enter the realm of the avatars, find software to make avatars and avatar worlds, study the avatar phenomenon, and read others' musings about the scene.

If these links don't do it for you, just go to Internet ➤ AOL Netfind and search for **avatar chat**. You'll find enough to keep you busy for quite a while...

NEWSGROUPS' LITTLE SECRET

Newsgroups are like AOL's message boards, but they're out on the Internet. A person will leave a message, and anyone can come by, read it, and respond to it.

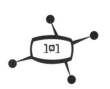

To get to newsgroups, go to keyword **newsgroups**. The Newsgroups window, shown in Figure 3.9, is mostly self-explanatory. The big tip here is that AOL's default doesn't give you access to *all* newsgroups, but you can change that (and no, changing it doesn't violate your TOS agreement).

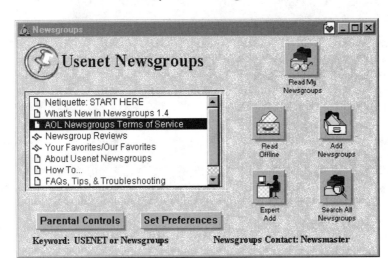

FIGURE 3.9:   Message boards for all can be found here.

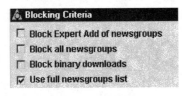

To give yourself access to all Internet newsgroups, follow these easy steps:

1. Make sure you're logged on as the master account screen name.

2. In the Newsgroups window, click Parental Controls.

3. Choose which screen name to edit Parental Controls for.

4. Uncheck Block Binary Downloads.

5. Check Use Full Newsgroups List.

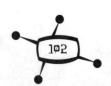

Now you'll have access to the entire newsgroup list (both AOL and Internet) and be able to download files posted on the newsgroups.

NOTE

Read the AOL Newsgroups Terms of Service, which you can find in the list on the left of the main Newsgroups window. In it you will see that, though you're about to fly freely through the Internet, you're still an AOL member and thus bound by AOL's rules.

MAILING LISTS

Mailing lists are a lot like newsgroups except that the messages come to your mailbox. At keyword **mailing list** you'll find AOL's directory of mailing lists out there. These aren't all the mailing lists that exist, just the ones AOL members have discovered. AOL doesn't police the lists, so there aren't any blocks to unblock here.

When you sign up for a mailing list, you'll get e-mail from everyone who discusses the list topic via the list. When you respond to the list, your e-mail goes out to every list member. The same rules of courtesy apply here as everywhere else.

TIP

Consider signing up for a *digest* of the mailing list you're interested in. Digests are compilations of each day's mailings into one e-mail (you'll be able to distinguish these because the mailing list name will include the word *digest* or *archive*). Otherwise, you'll be buried.

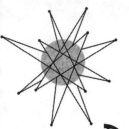

PROTECTING YOURSELF

Spam is that pinkish lumpish meat byproduct that shows up in your mailboxes, either as obnoxious or rude e-mail, or just as a lot of it (such as an advertisement flung indiscriminantly out to many different message boards and mailboxes).

You don't want it; what can you do?

Nix the member profile Basically, now that I've told you all about how to advertise who you are and find all the public places on AOL and the Internet, I'm going to tell you that the Number One way to avoid unwanted e-mails and IMs is: don't create a member profile.

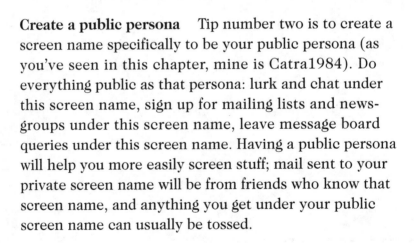

Create a public persona Tip number two is to create a screen name specifically to be your public persona (as you've seen in this chapter, mine is Catra1984). Do everything public as that persona: lurk and chat under this screen name, sign up for mailing lists and newsgroups under this screen name, leave message board queries under this screen name. Having a public persona will help you more easily screen stuff; mail sent to your private screen name will be from friends who know that screen name, and anything you get under your public screen name can usually be tossed.

Be nice One last tip, which as the sophisticated netizen you are you already know: Be polite in chat rooms. It's the best way to avoid a barrage of IMs and e-mails telling you to take it where the sun don't shine.

If you've been spammed, forward the e-mail, whether it's with an attachment or without, to **TOSemail1**.

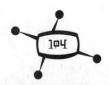

YOUR SNERT RECOURSE RESOURCE

You can make it really easy to report snerts (chat cretins) if you make a log of your chat session. When you create a log, you save everything that goes on in a given session so you can look back on the stuff that happened throughout your time online. Chat screens themselves only show a certain amount of the text, so you very quickly lose sight of the precious tidbits and belly-aching humor of the first lines.

To create a chat log:

1. Go to My Files ➤ Log Manager.

2. If you want to log everything you do other than chatting, choose Open Log under Session Log (see Figure 3.10).

3. If you just want to log your chat room antics, go to a chat room.

4. Now that you're in a chat room, the options under Chat Log will be active; choose Open Log there.

5. Choose a name for your log file in the Windows dialog box that comes up and press Save. As long as you keep the chat window open (minimized is okay), AOL will log the goings-on. You can participate or go elsewhere.

6. When you're done with your session, stop the logging by pressing Close Log.

7. Whether or not you're logged on, you can read the session by choosing File ➤ Open from AOL.

8. If you want to append an earlier log file, click Append Log and double-click the file you wish to append in the Append Log dialog box.

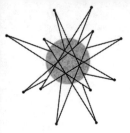

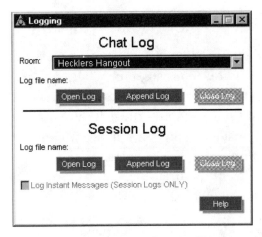

FIGURE 3.10: Log files: just like taping your favorite TV show while you're at dinner with your parents, except you can skip the dinner with your parents part.

WARNING

Remember to delete chat logs you don't want, lest your hard drive drown in drivel.

TIP

If a log file ends up being too big for AOL to open—about 32K plus—launch Notepad or Wordpad and open it from there.

To report a chat room snert:

1. Type **TOS** into the Keyword/URL box and press Go.

2. At the Terms of Service window, choose Report a Violation.

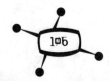

3. Click Chat.

4. Copy and paste the snerty words into the appropriate box, type in the snert's screen name, and what chat room you were in when the snerting occurred.

Unwanted AOL Mail

Those announcements; the modem, the visa, the add-on software...the list goes on. And on. You've seen them, clicked No Thanks a million times, and really, really would just like to log on. Please. If it wouldn't be too much to ask.

Marketing

To rid yourself of those commercial pop-ups, go to My AOL ➤ Preferences ➤ Marketing and double-click Tell Us What Your Pop-Up Preferences Are. (In AOL 3.0, go to keyword **marketing preferences**.)

Checkmarking the box at the lower right will turn off most pop-ups. As the disclaimer says, you'll still see a few pop-ups related to stuff AOL has got to tell you, but believe me, it cuts down on 99% of the advertising you slog through now.

MACROS AND PUNTS

Odds are, even if you've never chatted on AOL before, your first experience in a chat room will introduce you to macros and punting. Punts—kicking others off AOL—are often preceded by macros, multiline streams of chat lines generated from punt software. Punting is illegal on AOL but rampant. Macros are not illegal but are annoying when used to excess.

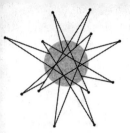

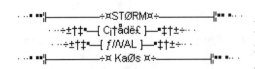

Macros can be benign, like 5-line-deep ASCII faces, or they can be mildly demonic-looking lines of text with accents littered about, looking like some strange other-worldly language.

Punters, on the other hand, can target you and freeze your screen so you have to reboot. That's when irritating becomes downright enraging.

If you get punted, copy down the screen name, reboot, and report it to the TOS Violations Community Action Team. To do so:

1. Type **TOS** into the Keyword/URL box and press Go.

2. At the Terms of Service window, choose Report a Violation.

3. Click Other, then choose IM Violations.

4. In the Cut and Paste a Copy of the IM box, type the offender's name and **IM punt**.

Now that you've met some folks and gotten comfortable with the AOL community, let's play some games!

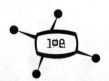

Chapter 4

Playing Premium Games

On our civilized society there's very little opportunity to experience the real-world challenges and adrenaline rushes of days past. No mountain lions threaten your commute to school or the office, you don't have to hunt down a bison during your lunch break to make sure you eat a decent meal at dinner, and you're not constantly on guard against attack by a neighboring tribe (well, depending on what part of the city you live in). Thank goodness for games to keep these challenges alive!

AOL offers some excellent games to hone your hunting skills and while away the hours; this chapter will tell you how to get the most out of the online multiplayer games.

Oh yeah, and for those of you who *prefer* a tigerless existence, there are logic and puzzle games to exercise your cerebral cortex.

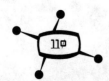

WHAT YOU SHOULD KNOW BEFORE YOU PLAY

Basically what you should know is that the online multiplayer games cost. Because extra money is involved, I'm going to spend some time up front talking about the lay of the pay-to-play land: how much you're being charged, how you know when you're racking up charges, what you're *not* charged for, and how to best prepare yourself to dive right into the games.

After you've been thoroughly briefed, I'll give you the low-down on the games plus some basics to help you decide which one you want to attack first.

THE PREMIUM ON PREMIUM GAMES

So where do you find the coolest games on AOL? There are plenty cool games at keyword **games** (also reachable through Channels ➤ Games), but the interactive multiplayer games, which are, yes, the *premium* games, are at keyword **worldplay** (Figure 4.1).

Premium games cost money, to wit (as of this writing):$1.99 per hour on top of your usual connect-time cost. You are only charged for the amount of time you play games, so fractions of hours will run ya 3.3 cents a minute. If you're on the unlimited access plan and something of a dilettante, this is no biggie. But if you're on the limited-access plan or you're hooked on multi-player online games, playing premium games is no small change.

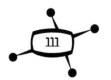

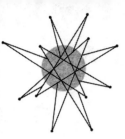

FIGURE 4.1:   Your bouncing-off point to the stars, the pool table, another age...

SECRET

Multiplayer games—including AOL's premium games and more—can be played online for a reasonable price (a flat fee of about $10 per month) at GameStorm's Web site: http://www.gamestorm.com.

WHEN THE CLOCK STARTS TICKING...

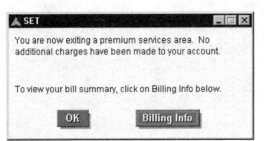

You'll always be greeted by a blue dialog box before you enter a premium area, and a pleasant little dialog box will bid you farewell.

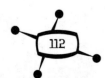

? Display Your Current Bill Summary To keep tabs on your tab, either click the Billing Info button in the above dialog box, or go to keyword **billing** and click the Display Your Current Bill Summary button. These charges may take a little time to process on AOL's end, therefore may not show up on your statement immediately.

NOTE

If your session gets interrupted and you lose paid playing time trying to extricate yourself from a premium game, go to keyword **credit** to report the problem and get the time/money credited to your account.

GETTING TO THE GAMES

There are two things you'll need to do to get into a game; you'll need to make sure your screen name has access to premium games, and you'll need to download the game to your hard drive. Instructions follow forthwith.

ENSURING SUBACCOUNT ACCESS

First off, you should know that subaccounts are automatically blocked (through AOL default) from accessing premium games, so if you wish to play under a playful screen name (or if you want to give your kid access to these games for a special treat), you'll need to unblock premium games for that screen name. To do so:

1. Sign on as the master account screen name and, in AOL's toolbar, go to My AOL ➤ Parental Controls.

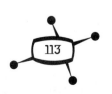

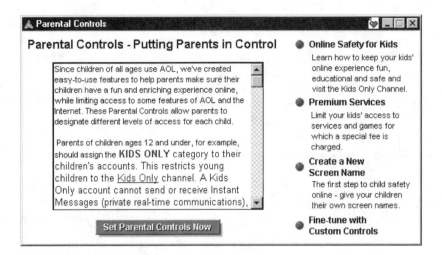

2. Click the Premium Services button on the right.

3. Notice that the master screen name has access to all premium services and the subaccount is blocked (poor Catra). Just click the checkbox to clear it and give that screen name access to premium games.

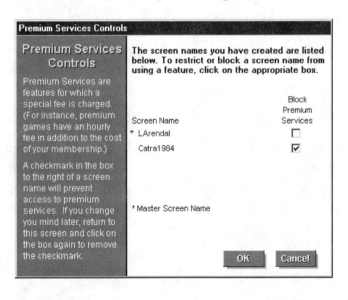

4. Click OK.

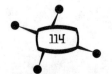

Downloading Each Game

Before you can play a game, you'll need to download it from AOL to your hard drive.

NOTE

The time it takes to download a game is, of course, not charged (unless you're on a limited-access plan). Depending on what game you're downloading and how fast your modem is, downloads can take anywhere from 30 minutes to 2 hours.

To download a game:

1. From the WorldPlay Games main screen's game list, double-click the name of the game. (You can also access it from the Game Categories list, of course.)

2. Click the wiggly PLAY button on the left.

3. The resultant dialog box, shown in Figure 4.2, will tell you what system requirements the game has and, usually, what the download time will be. To download the game, click the Free Download button on the right. (Notice that if you've already downloaded the game, you can go right to it with the Play Baldies—or SET or Air Warrior...—button.)

    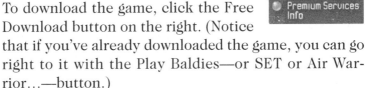

4. Click I Agree to acknowledge that you are entering a Premium Area (though, as you're performing a download, the dialog box notes that you won't be charged for your time).

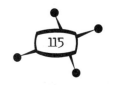

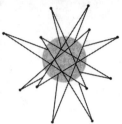

Go right into gameplay   Download the game

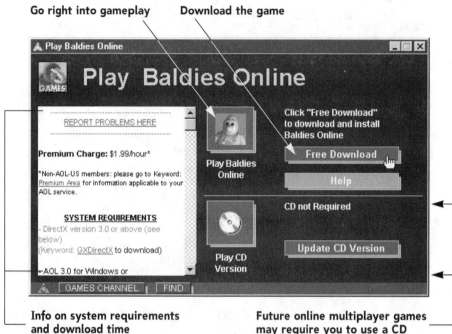

Info on system requirements   Future online multiplayer games
and download time   may require you to use a CD

FIGURE 4.2:   Your gateway to big fun

5. The AOL Installer will come up with a directory path for the game to be downloaded to. If you want to put it elsewhere (for instance, if you have a directory reserved for games), just click the Change button and navigate to the folder you wish to use (Figure 4.3). Note that once you get to the folder, you'll need to click the Create Dir button and type in a subfolder name (e.g., **Baldies**) for a complete path to be created. When you are satisfied with the download path, click OK once in the Game/ New Path dialog box and again in the AOL Installer dialog box.

6. The download will begin. You can go elsewhere in AOL (except another premium area) while you're waiting for the game to be downloaded and installed, or you can do something else on your computer—or you can catch up on your homework…

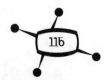

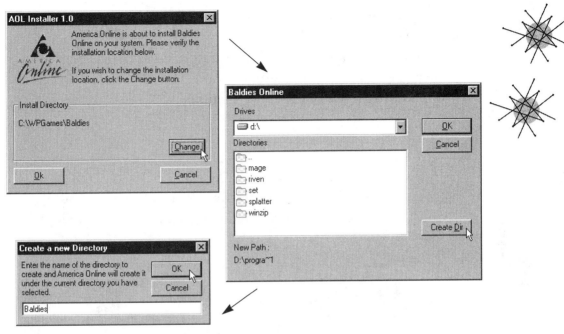

FIGURE 4.3: You may change the download directory during installation.

7. When the download is done, the game will usually launch itself. Don't worry if it can't find your AOL connection this time; just exit the game, then relaunch it from the WorldPlay Games area.

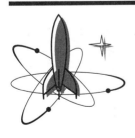

TIP

Most games you can try in single-player mode before you open yourself up to heated competition/being shot at. To do the single-player thing, you can either take advantage of that first non-connected launch to play around, or you can exit AOL and start the game from your hard drive. Much of the functionality will be disabled in the single-player version, but you'll get a feel for the controls and the look of the game.

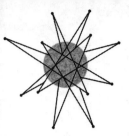

GETTING THE MOST OUT OF YOUR GAME TIME

Before you launch full steam and full price into your chosen game, check out the different options you have for getting comfortable with the rules and regulations.

THE RULES

First, look at the Help files for FAQs and rules for each game. You can access these from the main WorldPlay Games screen (click on Help) or from the individual game's area (click on How to Play).

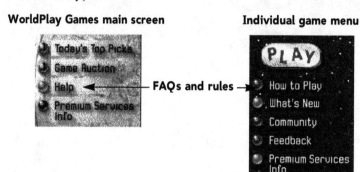

WorldPlay Games main screen

- Today's Top Picks
- Game Auction
- Help ← **FAQs and rules** →
- Premium Services Info

Individual game menu

PLAY
- How to Play
- What's New
- Community
- Feedback
- Premium Services Info

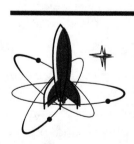

TIP

Especially note how to quit a game during play. You may be able to click the Windows 95 Close button or, just as easy, press the Esc key—or you may need to wait until combat is over, then type **quit**…. The point is, how to quit varies with the game, and you'll want to make sure you know how to end your game session so you don't waste time and money figuring it out.

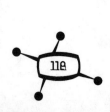

Quick Start Instructions

Some games are the play-and-learn type (you'll find this more in the puzzle and card game categories); these offer a Quickstart file. Here you can get a general feel for the game and then hone your skills by playing. The Quickstart approach is useful if you're the impatient type who'd rather figure out strategy on your own.

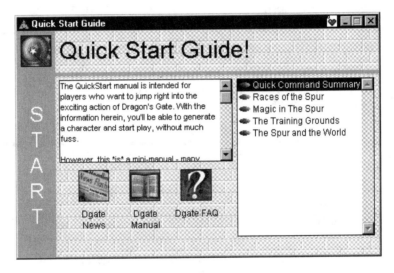

Coaching Corner

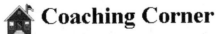

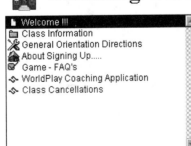

Especially if you're a beginner, you may want to take a breather in the Coaching Corner, also accessible from the WorldPlay Games main screen. Coaching will be more meaningful if you've played a game already, but it won't hurt to get some coaching

before sallying forth if you're particularly nervous about a game or your bank account. Coaching Corner offers a lot of beginner classes, with the promise of more advanced classes to come.

Game Chat Rooms and Message Boards

And don't forget the ever-present AOL community; if you have specific questions about a game (or specific tips you want to share with other gamesters), drop into the game chat rooms or leave a message on the appropriate WorldPlay Games message board; helpful staff members patrol these boards and will answer your query in good time. Reach the chat room and message boards by clicking the Community button, found in the list on the left of each game's main area.

Good Clean Fun

As in all areas of AOL, rules of courtesy are important to abide by. Please use inoffensive language and images in chat areas, game play, and profile information; treat others with respect (in other words, no harassment, no scrolling, no impersonating other members); and resist the temptation to send chain letters or solicit other players.

In addition, when posting to message boards please post in English, English being AOL Land's official language.

Both the paid and unpaid Games areas are patrolled by staff members intent on keeping the peace, so breaking the above rules is not without consequence.

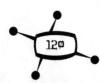

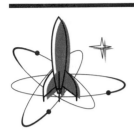

TIP

Speaking of community, an excellent way to find your way around the strange worlds here at WorldPlay is to find a mentor—a gamester with a lot of experience and patience—to guide you through the rough spots and find ways for you to gain experience points yourself. (This usually seems to involve finding an easy target for you to take on. Blood-thirsty bunch, these gamers...) As you move up in rank, don't forget to give back to the community what you got and look after those newbies.

Watch the Experts

For certain of the card and board games you can supplement the above learning methodologies by using the Watch option. Once you choose your card or board game, you'll notice a game table in the upper-right corner; if you wish to watch others rather than play, click the Watch button just above the game table. If Watch is inactive, either it isn't available for the game you've chosen, or the players of that particular round have opted to play in peace. (I'll show you how to set your options later in this chapter.)

WARNING

Just because you're watching doesn't mean you're not racking up those pennies.

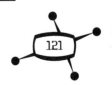

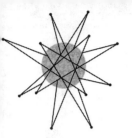

Test Drive a Beta Game

Lastly, a great way to play these excellent games for free is to test drive the new premium games. Find out what games are still in beta at keyword **gc test drive**. Keep in mind that *beta* means *buggy*, so you may crash in the process of play, but you won't get charged a penny for your playing time. Use the bug report forms for any problems that come up during play of a beta game.

Help!

If you need technical help with the games area, go to keyword **games help** for games tech support and try the support options shown at left.

TIP

If you have trouble launching the game you want, try exiting all the way out of the Premium Games area and then going back in. If you get a dialog box proclaiming "Server not found," it means the game is down, probably for servicing or upgrading. Try again later.

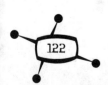

PLACES TO GO, PEOPLE TO MEET, GAMES TO PLAY

The Premium Games area offers a small but expanding selection of online multiplayer games, from adventurous fast-twitch fun to pensive logic-centered puzzles. Current offerings include:

Adventure Games	Strategy and Action	Classic Card	Puzzle & Board
Darkness Falls	Air Warrior II	Bridge	Backgammon
Dragon's Gate	Baldies Online	Gin	CatchWord
Legends of Kesmai	Harpoon Online	Hearts	Cribbage
Rolemaster: Magestorm	Heavy Damage	Online Casino	SET
	MultiPlayer BattleTech	Spades	Spunky's Shuffle
	Splatterball	Whist	The Incredible Machine 3
	Warcraft II		Virtual Pool

WHAT YOU CAN GENERALLY EXPECT

Here's what to expect when you enter the games. There are some common elements to the action adventure games and to the card and board games, so under each category I outline the basic steps you'll take to get yourself in on a game.

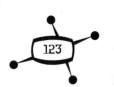

Adventure and Strategy & Action Games

Taking Magestorm as an example, here's how you get into your basic action adventure:

1. Go to keyword **worldplay**.

2. Choose your game from the scroll-able list in the middle of the main WorldPlay Games screen.

3. Click Play.

4. Click the Play *Game* button (Play Magestorm, in this example).

5. Click the I Agree button, acknowledging that you understand that you will be charged for using this area.

6. The game will launch and connect to AOL. At this point you'll be alone in the private foyer, which will take many shapes depending on the game (in Magestorm, it's a library; in Splatterball it's a small store). Figure 4.4 shows Magestorm's library; most of the options available here (viewable with ToolTips-like labels) are available in all the action adventure games.

7. Once you've created your character and configured your moves and location to your liking, enter the public foyer, shown in Figure 4.5. This may be called a tavern, as in Magestorm, or a clubhouse, like in Splatterball, or whatever game-appropriate title the creators have given it.

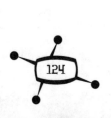

Exit Magestorm   **Create a new character**

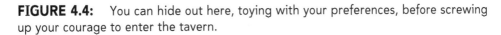

Enter the public   **View your**   **Configure your settings:**
foyer to Magestorm   **character's**   **keyboard controls, music**
                             characteristics   **and sound toggle, team**
                                                    affiliation, playing arena

FIGURE 4.4: You can hide out here, toying with your preferences, before screwing
up your courage to enter the tavern.

 8. From here you can peruse the list of current players and
   choose an existing venue for your excursion (by double-
   clicking on the place name in the Matches list) or create a new arena (by clicking the New button, selecting
   an arena and the levels allowed, and clicking Launch).

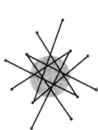

Closed to me because my character is a Level 1

Private match

Current open matches

List of current players with level, occupation, and whereabouts

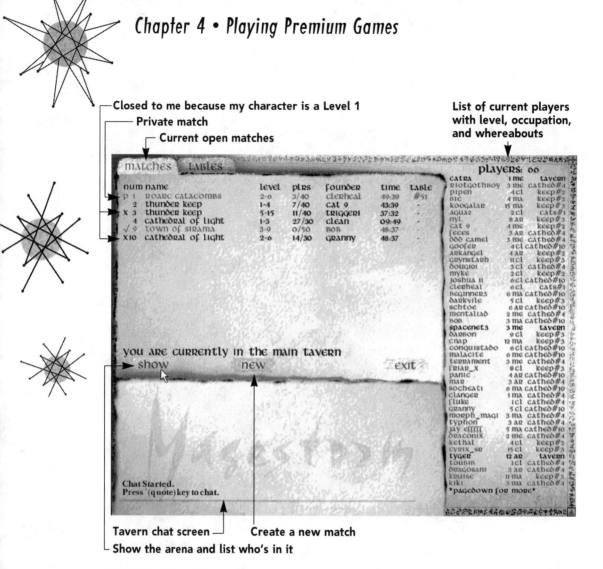

num	name	level	plrs	founder	time	table
p 1	roarc catacombs	2-6	3/40	clerheal	49:39	#51
2	thunder keep	1-4	7/40	cat 9	43:39	-
x 3	thunder keep	5-15	11/40	trigger1	37:32	-
4	cathedral of light	1-3	27/30	clean	09:49	-
√ 9	town of sirama	3-9	0/50	bob	48:37	-
x10	cathedral of light	2-6	14/30	granny	48:37	-

players: 66

catra	1 me	tavern
riotgothboy	3 me	cathed#4
pipen	4 cl	keep#2
bic	4 ma	keep#2
koogalar	15 ma	keep#3
agua2	2 cl	cats#1
nyl	8 ar	keep#3
cat 9	4 me	keep#2
feces	3 ar	cathed#4
666 camel	3 me	cathed#4
goofer	4 cl	cathed#10
arkangel	4 ar	keep#2
grynstarh	11 cl	keep#3
6ougioi	3 cl	cathed#4
myke	2 cl	keep#2
joshua 11	6 cl	cathed#10
clerheal	6 cl	cats#1
beginners	6 ma	cathed#10
6arkvile	5 cl	keep#3
schtoe	6 ar	cathed#10
mentaliad	2 me	cathed#4
bob	3 ma	cathed#10
spacenet3	3 me	tavern
6arbon	9 cl	keep#3
chap	12 ma	keep#3
conquistado	6 cl	cathed#10
malacite	6 me	cathed#4
terrament	3 me	cathed#4
friar_x	8 cl	keep#3
panic	4 ar	cathed#10
mar	3 ar	cathed#4
socheat1	6 ma	cathed#10
clanger	1 ma	cathed#4
fluke	1 cl	cathed#4
granny	5 cl	cathed#10
morph_magi	3 ma	cathed#4
typhon	3 ar	cathed#4
jay effff	5 ma	cathed#10
6raconix	2 me	cathed#4
kethal	4 cl	keep#2
cyrix_sr	15 cl	keep#3
tyger	12 ar	tavern
toubin	1 cl	cathed#4
6ragosan1	3 ar	cathed#4
kruise	11 ma	keep#3
kiki	3 ma	cathed#4
pagedown for more		

you are currently in the main tavern

show   new   exit

Chat Started.
Press '(quote)key to chat.

Tavern chat screen

Create a new match

Show the arena and list who's in it

FIGURE 4.5: There's a lot going on in this magical world.

9. Once in, the other players will be alerted to your arrival. The screen will look something like Figure 4.6 (the particular graphics will change according to the game, but the layout's the same). Play on!

10. When you're ready to quit, use the magic keystroke(s) you learned from the Help files (Magestorms' is the Esc key) and confirm your desire to exit. At this point you'll be able to view your billing information if you wish.

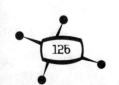

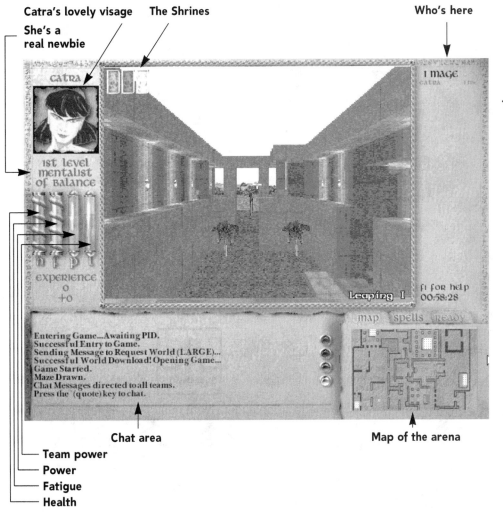

Catra's lovely visage

She's a real newbie

The Shrines

Who's here

Chat area

Map of the arena

Team power
Power
Fatigue
Health

FIGURE 4.6: Leaping about in the Temple of Ramhotep

Classic Card and Puzzle & Board Games

Follow these easy instructions to start a card or board game (for instance, SET) or certain action games (like Baldies Online):

1. Go to keyword **worldplay**.

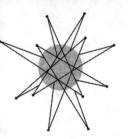

2. Choose your game from the scrollable list in the middle of the main WorldPlay Games screen.

3. Click Play.

4. Click the Play *Game* button (for instance, Play SET).

5. Click the I Agree button, acknowledging that you understand that you will be charged for using this area.

6. The game will launch and connect to AOL. You can read through the Getting Started dialog boxes, or just click the Close button.

7. Create a profile and character image for yourself by clicking the My Profile button; you can customize a female or male figure (Figure 4.7), or you can choose from the large variety of images in the Image Library. Add interests and background, and you may find like souls at your playing table (Figure 4.8).

8. Select a room to enter by double-clicking on a room in the room list. You'll have a choice of beginner to advanced, special events, coaching, and game-specific challenges.

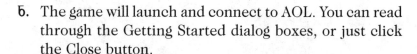

9. If you're the only occupant, click New Game to start. If there are others playing, click Select a Current Game to join that group. If there's an opening at the table, you'll see an empty chair around the playing table in the upper-right corner. Click it to join; the game will start when all the chairs are filled.

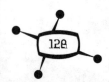

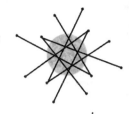

Looking at LArendal

Info | Game Skills | Interests | My Image

○ Build Image
○ Image Library

Features

Male/Female
Width
Skin Tone
Hair Color
Hair Style
Facial Hair

OK   Cancel

FIGURE 4.7: You could take the vaguely human route, not that anyone will believe you really look like this.

Looking at LArendal

Info | Game Skills | Interests | My Image

Handle: LArendal   Age: 1

City: Cayuga Lake   State: NY

E-Mail: Catra1984@aol.com

Bio: Born in an aquarium, I now live in a thriving community on beachfront property. I like swimming, sleeping, thinking, eating, and interacting with the other members of my community.

Interests: Hottubbing, Snorkeling, Surfing, Water skiing

Complain

OK   Cancel

FIGURE 4.8: Or you could go for total absurdity.

NOTE

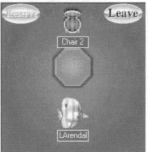

If you're invited to join a game, click the inviting player's name or image, and the game's table and chairs will appear.

10. To start a new game, click New Game. The Create Game Table dialog box will appear. From here, choose the number of players and click the Options button.

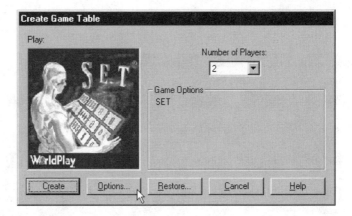

11. The Options dialog box gives you several tabs within which you can configure your game. The Summary tab is unexciting, so I'm going to skip directly to the General tab, shown in Figure 4.9.

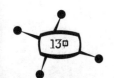

View game summary, add notes, or complain
Reserve specific chairs
Set game variations

Reservation options —
in case of quitters

How patient you —
want to be

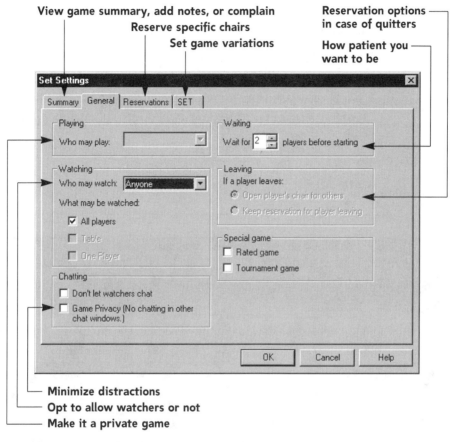

Minimize distractions
Opt to allow watchers or not
Make it a private game

FIGURE 4.9: Generally speaking, the options

12. The Reservations tab allows you to reserve a spot for a friend; at the tab, select the chair you wish to reserve, click the Reserve button, click the By Name radio button, and type in your friend's screen name. Check the spelling, click Reserve, and

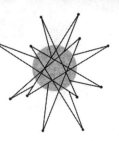

move on to the SET tab. The empty chair at your playing table will be tipped, with a note that it is reserved
for your friend.

13. At the SET tab, choose the type of game you wish to
play, then click OK. (Once a game has started, you can
change the game options from the Control Panel, which
is located on the Chat screen.)

14. When all players required are present, the game will
start. All games have a way to chat with other players,
as you see in Figure 4.10.

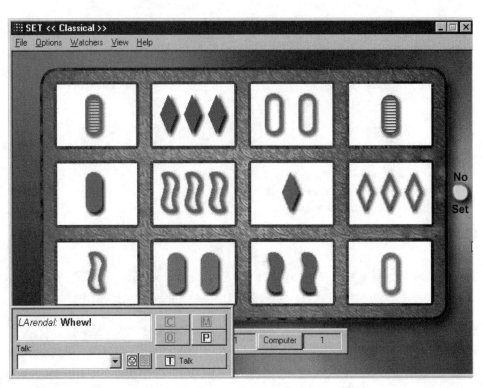

FIGURE 4.10: It's a computer-eat-player world in here.

15. When you're played out, click Exit, then Quit to leave the premium area.

16. Click OK (or view your Billing Info) to acknowledge the end of the paid playing session.

That's all I can tell you in terms of general hints; message boards and chat rooms can be really excellent ways to get the individual attention you need to feel comfortable with a game.

The Games

In this section I'm going to attempt to briefly synopsize all the online multiplayer games available on AOL so far. I'm not going to rate them; if you like it, it rocks. If you don't, it rocks for someone else. So I'll leave taste up to the individual. Here goes (alphabetically)…

Air Warrior II

Get yourself an aircraft, gas up and check yer ammo, and you're on! Fly around (skillfully, of course) and strafe everyone else without getting strafed.

Backgammon

You've all played Backgammon (okay, not all, but most of you have); it's a two-player game. After setting up your 15 pieces in Backgammon's special configuration, you roll dice and move your pieces off the board into your home trough, trying to block your opponent when possible.

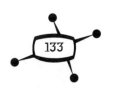

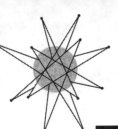

TIP

If you're a Backgammon beginner, keep Voices (the narrator) on to aid you in figuring out the rules.

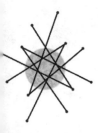

Baldies Online

You've got these little bald guys in red suits, and you want to set them to building, researching, and inventing. Don't forget to set some to soldiering so the non-red baldies can't get you. Basically, you want to get *them*. The most offensive group of baldies wins the day.

Some helpful, if bald, hints:

 Right-click on anything you want to know more about; the Baldy Help Advisor will describe it and maybe give you a few tips on it.

 Check your opponents' progress with the mini-map.

Taunt non-red baldies. Finally, that practice at Heckler's Online comes in handy!

Bridge

Bridge is the 4-person game our parents and grandparents played, teaming off against each other across a flimsy foldout card table late into the night. Thirteen cards each are dealt out, then the madness ensues. Basically a game of bluff and call-the-bluff, with super-complicated rules, Bridge is a game you'll want to watch for a while to get the hang of.

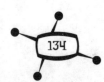

WorldPlay offers several Bridge variations for your bidding and tricking pleasure: Chicago (Standard, Cavendish, or Duplicate), Rubber, No Score, and Whist.

NOTE

If WorldPlay doesn't satisfy your Bridge urges, try keyword **bridge**.

CatchWord

Kind of a time-pressured Scrabble, you play CatchWord by watching letters appear on the playing board and using them to form a word (found in the dictionary, not a proper noun, etc.) of at least four letters in length. You can also steal words from other players by using the word plus new letters to form another word, and, of course, you can challenge others' words.

Cribbage

Two to four players play this blackjack-like card & board game; after the cards are dealt, players lay down cards just short of or equal to 31 points. Pegs are moved around the Cribbage board in relation to a complex system of rules based on what cards and combinations of cards were played in the hand. The first player to move 121 spaces wins.

There is no inviter option in WorldPlay's Cribbage, so whoever graces your online table is who you'll play.

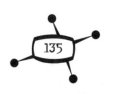

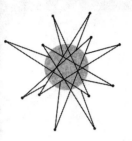

Darkness Falls

 You may have thought that you've been doing all sorts of dark, evil things in other games, but not compared to what you'll do in Darkness Falls. It's a role-playing game where your only character choices are evil, to be played to the darkest ends in a decaying virtual town. If you've ever secretly longed to be a skeleton, zombie, demon, werewolf, vampire, or shady human, Darkness Falls is your place to explore that side of you while fighting and training to advance your skill level.

Dragon's Gate

Dragon's Gate is a role-playing adventure game involving magic, combat, middle-ages sort of stuff. You know. Advance your skills to advance your rank, casting spells and fighting foes to keep alive.

Useful things to know:

 Type **help** to see a list of commands. Type a command and press Enter to get a description of what the command will accomplish and how to use it.

 Use **set info** (type **set info help** for list of commands) to control how much information you get about the action around you.

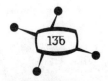

Gin

A two-person card game involving melding (much like Hearts or Canasta) and going out (declaring *gin*) before your opponent. A succession of games is played until one player has 100 points. WorldPlay offers the following variations: Oklahoma and Hollywood Gin.

WorldPlay's Gin also offers a training mode, where the dealer decides who gets what card to help along the novice.

Harpoon Online

 Join or create a team to do aquatic battle with your enemies and, with your modern and (virtual) naval weapons, prevent them from controlling the world's oceans before you do.

NOTE

Though Harpoon Online is quite difficult to learn, it's totally worth it if this type of game is your bag.

Hearts

Three to five players play, each of you trying to score fewer points than your opponents do. After your cards are dealt, discard frantically (but according to the rules)—especially your hearts—to win.

NOTE

GameStorm's card games can be found at keyword **classic cards**.

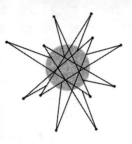

Heavy Damage

Flying your futuristic hover-craft through a virtual maze, you must search out and destroy as many other heavy-damage-wannabes as possible, all the while defending your-self from attack by same. Complete with hipster vocab (frag or be fragged, baby!) and an arsenal to drool over, Heavy Damage packs enough action into its rules alone to get your adrenaline going.

Legends of Kesmai

Another role-playing game where you fight other characters to win points and influence, umm, the level-escalating forces that be. Medieval.

NOTE

Note that in addition to the usual Legends of Kesmai game download, you also need to download ODBC (database tools) and DirectDraw. These are available from the Legends of Kesmai How to Play area.

Multiplayer BattleTech

Based on MechWarrior, in BattleTech you travel to where the action is and unload your weapons into your choice of other online players or droids.

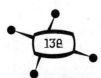

NOTE

You can get a walk-through tutorial of the BattleTech way of life from the Solaris Starport Arrivals area.

Online Casino

You've got your choice of Five Card Stud, Five Card Draw, Seven Card Stud, Texas Holdem, or Omaha Holdem here at the online casino. The vocabulary will be familiar to you stone-faced Reno-goers; for you greenhorns, look under the Help menu for the rules.

Rolemaster: Magestorm

A magical role-playing game of capture the shrine (rather, blow up all shrines belonging to orders other than your own to capture an arena) and kill or be killed, get resurrected or die, bias pools of earthblood (don't ask) toward your own order...

Set

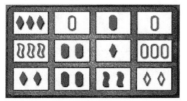

Singly, against the computer, or against up to seven other players, you can take on this pack of cards and show it who's boss. You have to match the card patterns in sets of three before your opponent(s) find the match. Said match can be of similar features or dissimilar features.

I recommend watching before playing; it takes a while to get used to the cards.

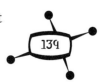

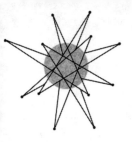

Spades

Spades is a three- or four-person card game involving bids and tricks, the objective of which is to earn the highest number of points. Read the rules.

Splatterball

 It's virtual paintball, much less dangerous than the human-interface real-life kind in that big room where the ceiling's sometimes blue and sometimes black… Create a character, join a team, and splat as many opponents with your paint gun as you can. Capture the flag and bring it to your team's home base to gain points.

On one of the rare occasions you aren't online, power up Splatterball and practise running and splatting in single-user mode.

Spunky's Shuffle

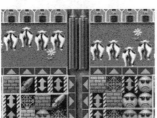 This new game pits you against either the computer or against another online player as you struggle to align your tiles toward your goal as well as to block your opponent.

It's colorful and it's silly! What more could you ask after a hard day of Heavy Damage or Dragon's Gate?

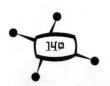

The Incredible Machine 3

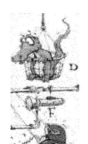

Brain teasers galore; choose a puzzle (which often involves getting something, like a bouncing ball, from one place to another) and place various gadgets in the puzzle field to build a moving or appropriately angled machine to solve said puzzle.

Some helpful hints:

 Use the spyglass to find out what a gadget is and does.

 If you've placed a gadget and nothing happens, you may need to connect another gadget to it to activate it.

Opponents might be friendly (chat with them for ideas) or malicious (bomb them before they bomb you), and it behooves you to find out which.

Virtual Pool

Pool is pool. A series of commands brings you a virtually realistic game of eight-ball, nine-ball, or rotation. Beer and brawling not provided.

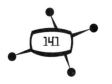

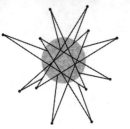

Warcraft II

Be you Human or Orc, your object is to crush the other. However, Warcraft II is not just a search-and-destroy game. You must feed your forces and harvest resources in order to strengthen your side. And *then* you can search out the Orcs (or Humans) and destroy them!

NOTE

Find online tournament schedules for your favorite games by following this path from WorldPlay Games' main screen: Today's Top Picks ➤ Events. Tournaments are held either in the WorldPlay Games Events Room or at Love@AOL, so be sure to check the location. Note that the listed times are Eastern Standard time; plan appropriately.

WHERE TO FIND FINE NONPREMIUM GAMES

The Games channel has game demos and reviews, which you can connect to from Games Central (from Playstation's Final Fantasy VII, Nintendo's Diddy Kong Racing, to obscure PC games like Manx TT Super Bike).

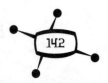

Where to Find Fine Nonpremium Games

If you're stuck in a game, any game (such as Riven) or you want cheat codes (for SimCity, for instance), post your request to the Games Insider community message boards. To get to the Games Insider community, go to keyword **games**, click Games Insider (on the left), and you're there. The message boards can be accessed from the list on the right: Games Central Messaging is the place.

The Game Insider area also brings you the Weekly Game news, updating you about new game happenings on AOL; the news archives give you past game reviews and news.

Other nonpremium game venues include Game Shows Online (at keyword **game shows**), which has a wide selection, or Antagonist, Inc. (keyword **ant**).

You can access the Online Gaming Forums at keyword **ogf**—forums include a freeform gaming forum, where you create a character and interact with other characters in a chat room to create a story, sim forum, strategy forum, collectible card games forum, chess forum, game designer's forum, wargaming forum—you name it, it could be there.

Be sure to check out NTN Games Studio (keyword **ntn**), which features a timed competitive trivia contest of 15 trivia questions per game. Check the daily schedule for different games.

Okay, enough fun and games. Now that you've performed a bunch of downloads and are familiar with the various amusements AOL has to offer, let's do a little sweeping and dusting. The next chapter features your Personal Filing Cabinet and all the little tricks you can use to keep your hard drive ambulatory.

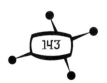

Chapter 5

Managing AOL: Secrets to Organize By

Organization is a personal thing; no two people organize their work files or school assignments the same way. Go into another person's kitchen, and you'll have to ask where the silverware drawer is. Do your T-shirts and turtlenecks go in the same dresser drawer? Do jeans get folded or hung up on hangers?

So far in this book I've taken you through e-mail, IMs, chat rooms, and games. You've no doubt received some legitimate (nonhacker) attachments that you've downloaded to your hard drive, and you've probably taken advantage of the tips I've given you on downloading cool sound files and AOL add-ons. In Chapters 6 and 7 I'll give you further hunting and gathering tips for finding what you want out there in AOL—and cyberspace. Now—while you have a few files but not so many that you're

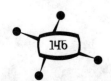

overwhelmed by it all (theoretically, anyway)—is a good time to think about keeping your e-mails, newsgroup messages, and downloaded files in order.

In this chapter I'm going to give you the tools for organizing and managing your AOL files, which will save you time and keep your hard drive happy and running as fast as it can. I'll also make suggestions along the way, which will hopefully help you figure out an organizational system that works for you.

YOUR PERSONAL FILING CABINET

Briefly, then, let me run through the basic Personal Filing Cabinet (PFC) features before going on to more complicated stunts. Figure 5.1 shows my PFC in its almost-pristine state. All the folders save the one selected are AOL folders; these AOL folders cannot be renamed, deleted, or moved around. Any folder you add to the PFC, like my AOL4 Stuff folder, can be customized to your greatest advantage.

MAIL AND YOUR PFC

The first thing you'll want to do is make sure your mail is making it into your PFC. I discussed this operation in Chapter 1, *Excelling in E-Mail*, but I'll touch on it here, too. There's nothing more discouraging than seeing your mail disappear from your Online Mailbox forever. To avoid that, follow these steps:

1. Sign on to AOL (setting some Mail Preferences must be done online).

2. From AOL's toolbar, choose My AOL ➤ Preferences.

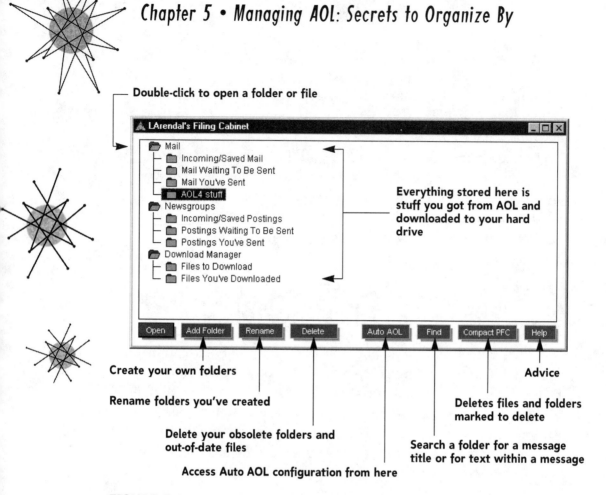

Double-click to open a folder or file

Everything stored here is stuff you got from AOL and downloaded to your hard drive

Create your own folders

Advice

Rename folders you've created

Deletes files and folders marked to delete

Delete your obsolete folders and out-of-date files

Search a folder for a message title or for text within a message

Access Auto AOL configuration from here

FIGURE 5.1: Slightly more attractive than the usual metal contraption, AOL's Filing Cabinet is your central organization system.

3. Click the Mail button.

4. Check the fourth and fifth options (shown below) as desired; these will save the mail you've written and/or save the mail you receive.

Mail

☑ Retain all mail I send in my Personal Filing Cabinet

☑ Retain all mail I read in my Personal Filing Cabinet

5. Click OK.

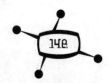

Everything you write, read, and download will automatically be saved in your PFC (downloaded files are automatically saved there; mail is the only thing that you must choose to save).

Now you need some good organizing and archiving schemas so your hard drive doesn't get overwhelmed.

TIP

Even with a highly pigeon-holed filing system, you'd still have to have a mind like a steel trap to remember where everything is. Luckily, AOL provides an excellent search tool right in the PFC window. To find your friend's e-mail about the karaoke party, click the Find button, and you'll be able to choose which folders to search and whether to search file titles or file text. And once you find the file you're looking for, you can use the Find in Top Window command (on the Edit menu) to find the passage you're thinking of.

MANAGING YOUR CLUTTER

The first thing you can do to make sense of the slew of e-mail and downloads you have is to organize them into folders. You can create subfolders under the following PFC folders:

Mail

Incoming/Saved Mail

Mail You've Sent

Newsgroups

Download Manager

Any folder you create

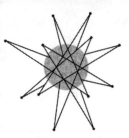

To create a folder, merely highlight the folder you wish to store the new folder under, click the Add Folder button, type in the new folder's name, and click OK. You might want to organize your mail by the person who sent it to you, by content (such as a project you're working on or jokes e-mailed to you), by date (for instance, everything sent in September), or a mix of all of these (such as in Figure 5.2). Or by a category I haven't thought of.

TIP

A folder I find quite useful is the Delete After Time Passes folder. I file time-sensitive stuff there, like invitations to parties, so I can refer back to an invite in case I forget how or when to get to the event. After the party, I won't need that specific message, so when I check this folder I can delete the invitation along with the other stuff I've already taken care of.

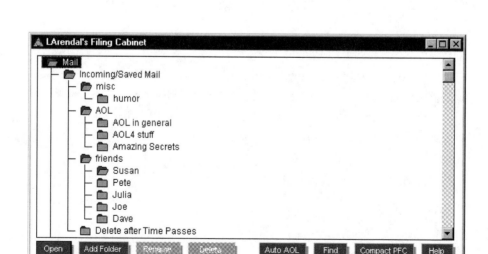

FIGURE 5.2: A well-categorized PFC can be the quiet café moment amidst the hustle and bustle of AOL.

Now that you've created your folders, you'll want to move your mail as appropriate. That's easy: just drag and drop.

Filing Many Messages with One Drag'n'Drop

As in Windows 95, you can select multiple files easily in your PFC: if they're contiguous, select the first one, hold down the Shift key, and select the last one. If the files are noncontiguous, choose them by holding down the Ctrl key and selecting each one you want to move. When all the files you want are highlighted, let go of the Shift or Ctrl key, click on one of the highlighted files, and drag'n'drop the bunch to the folder of your choice.

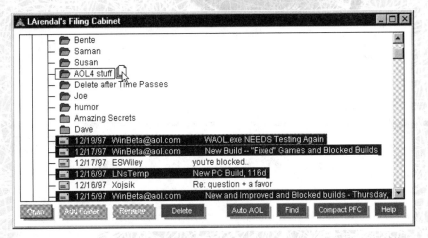

Say you have so many e-mails that, once you scroll down to a message you want to file, you can't see the folder you want to drop it into. Cut and Paste isn't available; what to do? No problem. Just right-click the folder you want access to and, from the right-click menu, choose New Window. The folder will open up

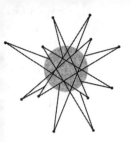

its own window, to which you can drag'n'drop messages from the first window. Figure 5.3 illustrates.

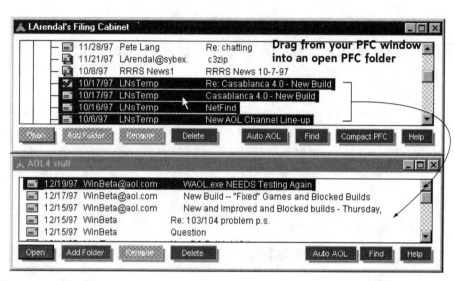

FIGURE 5.3: Arrange your two windows, select your files, and drag'n'drop.

THE SECRET TO GRACEFULLY REARRANGING FOLDERS

Unfortunately, it's not so easy to move PFC folders around. When you create folders, the new ones are just stacked on top of the older ones. If you try to drag'n'drop a folder in front of another folder, your selected folder will be absorbed by the folder that your dragging cursor highlights. There is no alphabetizing function, not that that's necessarily how you'd want to organize your PFC files anyway.

The only way to really shuffle your PFC folders is to drag'n'drop them again, in order, into their parent folder (this is the folder that

Continued

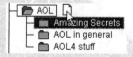

your PFC folders are subfolders of—in Figure 5.2, for example, the AOL folder is the parent folder to the Amazing Secrets, AOL4 Stuff, and AOL in General subfolders). What subfolder do you want at the beginning of the stack? Drag that one to its parent folder and drop it; it'll appear at the bottom. Don't be fooled, though, if you drag the subfolder you want to be second in line to the top, it'll drop to the bottom, right after the previously dragged'n'dropped folder. Repeat until your folders are in order.

DELETING UNWANTED CLUTTER

Another obvious thing you can do to maintain your filing sanity is to delete the messages and files you don't want. I know, you're thinking, "Well, duh! Just hit Delete!" It's almost that easy, but not quite. Following are a few things to keep in mind.

Thing 1   When you open up an e-mail message in your Online Mailbox, the message gets stored in your PFC. Even if you close the e-mail and click Delete, you will only have deleted it from your Online Mailbox. You will still have a copy stored in your PFC and will have to delete it from your PFC separately.

Thing 2   When you enter your PFC, highlight an e-mail message or file, and click Delete, the selected file disappears from your PFC screen *but has not yet actually been deleted*. Instead, it lurks in that dark corner of your hard drive reserved for files sent to the Recycle Bin and the AOL trash compactor.

Ergo thing 3   As you must empty Windows 95's Recycling Bin, you must Compact your PFC trash. To truly empty your hard drive of the files and messages marked

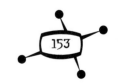
153

to be deleted from your PFC, click the Compact PFC button at the lower right of your PFC window. You don't need to Compact your trash every time you delete one little thing from your PFC, but you'll want to do it once in a while. And, if you don't want to think about it, you can instead rely on PFC Preferences to warn you when your PFC gets bigger than you want (see *Who Sez Size Doesn't Matter?* below for instructions).

Keep in mind that each screen name has its own PFC; therefore, you must be signed on as a particular screen name to organize and maintain its PFC.

TIP

Compact your PFC offline and when you're not going to use AOL for a while; sometimes it can take a while to get through the compacting process.

THE SECRET TO PURGING OUT-DATED SURFING SESSIONS

Each time you brave the tempestuous waves of cyberspace, you accumulate a trail that gets stored in your Temporary Internet Files folder. You'd be surprised at how much crap builds up there; those hotlinks that promised something exciting yet delivered something completely uninteresting get the same amount of legroom as your usual haunts.

Continued

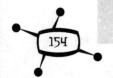

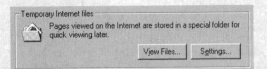

Check out your trail; from the toolbar, choose My AOL ➤ Preferences, click the WWW icon, and then click the Advanced tab. The middle field, Temporary Internet Files, is the one you want.

Click View Files—and look at the scads of hotlinks! Do you need them all? Absolutely not. Do you need *any* of them? Not really. They're useful in that when you revisit a Web site, AOL accesses the file stored in your Temporary Internet Files, checks against the real thing for changes, then displays an updated page (and stores it you know where). It does make the Web-page-loading process quicker. However, a stored page is a stored page, whether you ever access it again or not.

To purge yourself of these hotlink albatrosses, close out of your Temporary Internet Files folder (there's no Cancel button, so just click the Close button in the Title bar) and, back at the Advanced tab, click the Settings button.

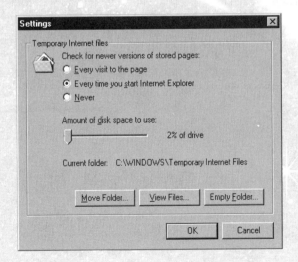

Continued

In the Settings dialog box you can adjust how much Internet garbage gets stored on your hard drive. If you've a huge hard drive and aren't cramming it with huge applications, you might not be worried about how much space is taken up by stored Web pages. If, on the other hand, you have a smallish hard drive or are naturally suspicious of anything that lurks in dark corners, you can rid yourself of your temporary Internet files by clicking the Empty Folder button. You'll want to make a habit of it.

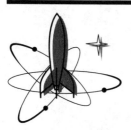

TIP

Speaking of outdated sessions, what about art associated with AOL's areas? Every time you boogie on over to a different AOL area, you're downloading the page, art and all, to your computer. AOL stores this art and, when you return to an area, AOL calls on its stored files to reinstate and update themselves. Thus, as with temporary Internet files, the area loads more quickly the second time around. However, online art does take up room on your hard drive. To manage this amount, choose My AOL ➤ Preferences and click the Graphics icon to get your Graphics Preferences dialog box.

WHO SEZ SIZE DOESN'T MATTER?

When you get your organization system set up, you'll want to maintain it so it doesn't become a disorganization system.

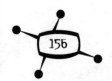

Check the size of each of your screen names' PFCs once in a while in Windows Explorer. Your PFC contents are stored under C:\America Online 4.0\Organize, as illustrated in Figure 5.4. Notice the numbers in the Size column? If they get too big (10MB or so), you'll want to go into your PFC (via AOL) and delete the old stuff.

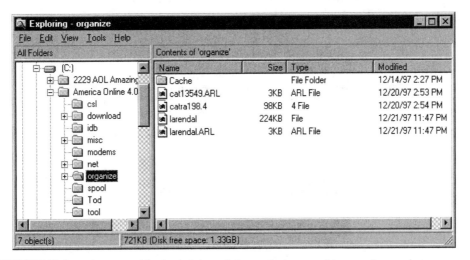

FIGURE 5.4: Catra and L. Arendal each have their own things going on here.

TIP

Because your PFC is stored on your hard drive, you can do anything PFC-related offline—as long as you're on your own computer.

Even better, automate the PFC-size check by setting your PFC preferences to warn you when your PFC reaches a size you deem unwieldy. To do so:

1. From the toolbar, choose My AOL ➤ Preferences.

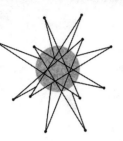

2. Click the Personal Filing Cabinet icon.

3. In the Personal Filing Cabinet Preferences dialog box (shown in Figure 5.5), choose your warning. You can choose to be notified if your PFC reaches anywhere from 1MB to 1000MB (you specify). You might also be interested in monitoring the percent of space that's available in your PFC (from 1 to 100, of course).

Personal Filing Cabinet

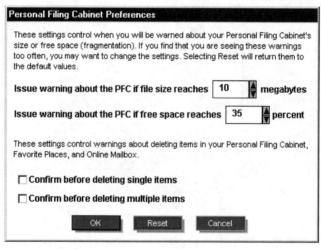

Personal Filing Cabinet Preferences

These settings control when you will be warned about your Personal Filing Cabinet's size or free space (fragmentation). If you find that you are seeing these warnings too often, you may want to change the settings. Selecting Reset will return them to the default values.

Issue warning about the PFC if file size reaches `10` **megabytes**

Issue warning about the PFC if free space reaches `35` **percent**

These settings control warnings about deleting items in your Personal Filing Cabinet, Favorite Places, and Online Mailbox.

☐ **Confirm before deleting single items**
☐ **Confirm before deleting multiple items**

[OK]   [Reset]   [Cancel]

FIGURE 5.5: AOL's default numbers give you a lot of closet space to ferret those files away.

NOTE

For some mysterious reason, AOL has stuck an important pair of mail preferences here. If you wish to confirm that you do indeed wish to delete the file you just pressed the Delete key to delete, you can set yourself up to receive exactly that confirmation dialog box right here. It could come in very handy if your finger accidentally slips one day and deletes the first e-mail your girlfriend ever sent you.

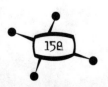

THE SECRET TO KEEPING YOUR DOWNLOADS MANAGEABLE

I'll go into downloads later in this chapter, but for now let me tip you off to yet another way to keep the size of your files down. Three words: keep 'em compressed.

To automate this option, set your preferences as follows:

1. In the toolbar, choose My AOL ➤ Preferences.

2. Click the Download icon.

3. In the Download Preferences dialog box, look closely at the second and third options.

Download

> ☑ Automatically decompress files at sign-off
>
> ☐ Delete ZIP files after decompression

4. If you download files willy-nilly, you'll want to uncheck the Automatically Decompress option. That way, you can download to your heart's content and decompress each file only when you actually want to use it.

5. If you're selective about the files you download and you never download something you aren't going to want to explore right away, keep Automatically Decompress checked. Consider also checkmarking the Delete ZIP Files After Decompression option. This way you'll have immediate access to your files, and you won't have the compressed versions bouncing around and taking up space.

If any of your files don't come already compressed or you want to compress them after playing with them a while, just download WinZip (I tell you how in Chapter 1) and zip those puppies up for safe storage.

ARCHIVING

Your PFC is only as good as your hard drive. If your hard drive goes, so goes your stored AOL e-mail, addresses, and down-loaded files (not to mention whatever non-AOL stuff you've got stored!). To prevent an electronic calamity from wiping out years of AOL accumulations, back up your files on floppies from time to time (or on zip disks or jaz drives—whatever!).

 To copy your Address Book to a floppy, drag'n'drop C:\America Online 4.0\idb\AddrBk.ind over to the A drive (once a disk is inserted, of course).

 To copy your PFCs to a floppy, drag'n'drop C:\America Online 4.0\ Organize to your A drive. This action will save all your screen names' PFCs: mail, newsgroup messages, and all.

Should you ever need to restore your PFCs or Address Book (which I certainly hope you never have to do), just insert the floppy with the most recent backup into your A drive and drag'n'drop the necessary files over to C:\America Online 4.0. Don't worry about replacing the existing Organize folder and AddrBk.ind; if you're restoring, it must be because the old ones don't exist anymore (perhaps a lightning storm required you to reinstall AOL, or perhaps you merely purchased a new computer).

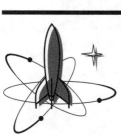

TIP

Another excellent way to flex your archiving muscle is to copy your entire PFC once a month, then delete all your files (or all your files save those you still need access to).

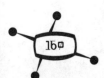

Managing All Those Downloaded Files

I've discussed the how-tos of and caveats around downloads and uploads extensively in Chapter 1, *Excelling in E-Mail*. But while we're honing our file-management skills, let's throw some download management in the mix.

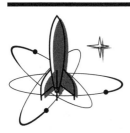

TIP

While you're downloading files, you can multitask—on AOL, on your computer, or in real life. Surf AOL, write a manifesto in Word, go out to a movie, go to sleep. Keep in mind, however, that memory hogs—like games—don't take kindly to sharing computer time with downloads.

You'll want to start managing downloads from the Download Preferences dialog box (Figure 5.6). Access it by choosing My AOL ➤ Preferences and clicking the Download button.

Download Preferences

☐ Display Image Files on Download

☑ Automatically decompress files at sign-off

☐ Delete ZIP files after decompression

☑ Confirm additions to my download list

☑ Retain information about my last `50` ▲▼ downloads

Use this directory as default for downloads:

`C:\FUNAOL~1`   Browse

OK   Cancel

FIGURE 5.6:   One batch of preferences, coming up!

The first option is self-explanatory—either you like to see pictures as they're downloaded or you don't—and I've already talked about the second and third options, so I'm going to skip to

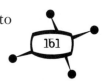

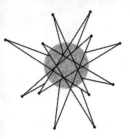

the last two possibilities in this box. What you do with the last option, which allows you to change your default download directory, may affect how you think about the second-to-last option, so I'll start from the bottom up.

Every time you download a file, you have the option to throw it into the default folder (the default being whatever directory is listed in this last field) or to designate another destination folder.

Here in the Preferences dialog box you can designate the folder in which you want to store downloads more often than not. AOL's default is C:\America Online 4.0\Download; you can take it or leave it. You'll notice I've chosen C:\Fun AOL Stuff to be my usual dumping ground.

However, you won't always put files in your default folder, so you might also want to keep a good number of downloads in your Download Manager's memory. That way, when you remember you saw that file *somewhere*, you can just go to My Files ➤ Download Manager, click the Show Files Downloaded button, find the file you want to get hold of, and click the Show Status button. One of the stats you'll be shown is the file's download directory. Look at it, remember it, go there, and you'll find it.

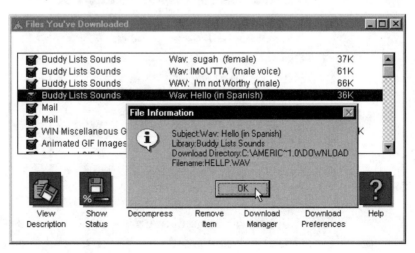

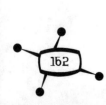

NOTE

If your download gets interrupted—or for some reason you click Finish Later in the File Transfer dialog box—you *could* begin the download from where you left off when you sign on again (go to My Files ➤ Download Manager, highlight the *filus interruptus*, and click Download). This may or may not lead to corrupted files. My advice is to start over, especially if you're downloading an .exe file.

ORGANIZING YOUR AOL TOOLBAR

Within certain limits you can customize your AOL toolbar. To start off, check out your options in the Toolbar Preferences dialog box:

1. From the AOL toolbar, go to My AOL ➤ Preferences.

2. Click the Toolbar icon.

3. In the ensuing Toolbar Preferences dialog box, shown in Figure 5.7, you can make some choices.

However, much more exciting is the added toolbar functionality you get when you set your monitor to 800x600 or higher resolution. If you have a 15" monitor or smaller, this resolution can be pretty hard on the eyes, but it's worth trying just to check out the expanded toolbar, which I've included here in Figure 5.8.

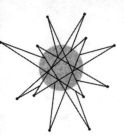

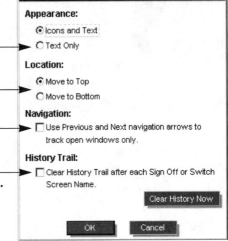

This option will make your toolbar quite small →

Do you want to read your menus from the top down or bottom up? →

If left unchecked, the toolbar's Previous and Next arrows will cycle through all windows you've been to, whether open or closed →

The History Trail can be accessed by clicking the Down arrow next to the Keyword/URL box. →

FIGURE 5.7: Some awfully useful options

NOTE

To set your monitor to a different resolution, right-click on your Windows 95 Desktop, choose Properties, and click the Settings tab. Here you can set your resolution and color display.

FIGURE 5.8: Everything looks smaller, but there's more of it.

Even though you'll go blind after staring at the compacted screen even for a short while, you'll be well-informed of your stock's performance and the weather anywhere in the world—not to mention, you can keep abreast of what perquisites AOL members are privy to.

THE REAL (SECRET) FUN WITH 800X600 RESOLUTION TOOLBARS

The ultimate in customizability is right here, under our 800x600 noses. Right-click on one of the last three toolbar icons: Quotes, Perks, or Weather. Notice that you have one option: Remove from Toolbar. Take the option and run with it; I'll show you why.

1. Remove one of the removable toolbar icons.

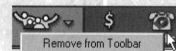

2. Go to a Favorite Place (or AOL area or Web site) that you'd like to have (you guessed it!) toolbar access to.

3. Drag the heart icon to the now-empty place in the toolbar; a Select Icon dialog box will pop up.

4. Select a pretty icon, type in a label (which will accompany the picture onto your toolbar), and click OK.

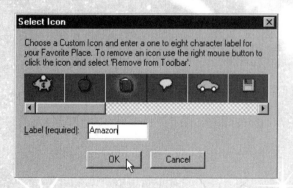

Continued

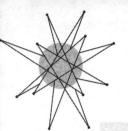

Your toolbar now proudly bears your very own link!

Amazon.com! Earth's Biggest Bookstore

Pretty cool, huh? You can replace any or all of the last three icons with your own choices. Now if only the whole toolbar were customizable at 640x480, we could all still see *and* we'd each have our own completely different AOL experience. But, hey, it's a start.

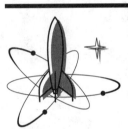

TIP

If you go to the same fave place every day anyway, why not sign on that way? To make it so, size your AOL window so you can see your Windows 95 Desktop, open up your Favorite Places, and drag'n'drop your favorite Fave out to your desktop. Whenever you want to sign on to AOL, double-click this Desktop icon, and AOL will start up for you. Just type in your password, and you're there.

Next stop, the Internet!

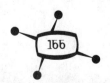

Chapter 6

Searching with Purpose

Finding what you want out there in cyberspace, whether the space is of the AOL or Internet variety, can be an exercise in frustration. Sometimes it seems like a whole exercise video workout in frustration; you think you've been clear, and it turns out a whole lot of Web pages or AOL areas fit the description you set forth.

The following pages will help you hone your searching skills—both on AOL and on the Web—and minimize extraneous and erroneous results to your searches.

SEARCHING WITHIN AOL

You'll be amazed at the quality and breadth of the stuff you'll find on AOL. Not only is it safe and warm here, there's lots to sift through. To make your sifting easier and more rewarding, you'll want to use the Find button.

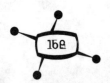

NOTE

Remember that using words to search is different from using a keyword to get somewhere. *Search words* can be anything describing an area or touched on within the area; a *keyword* is a word associated specifically with an area. If you tried to search for *HO*, you wouldn't find a thing. However, if you type **ho** into the Keyword/URL box and click Go, you'll immediately be connected to Heckler's Online. To successfully search for Heckler's Online, you'd need to search with a descriptive word like *humor*.

Easily accessed from the right side of the AOL toolbar, the Find button (Figure 6.1) allows you to search all of AOL or the Web, or narrow your search to AOL's channels, software area, chat rooms, member directory, access numbers, Help files, or the Internet White Pages.

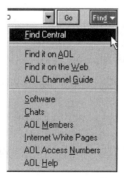

FIGURE 6.1: You have direct access to the search capabilities you're—ahem—searching for right here in the toolbar.

Even clearer than the Find menu is Find Central, the top-most menu item on the Find menu. Figure 6.2 illustrates your options for searching AOL.

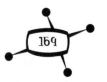

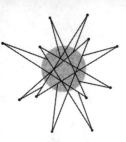

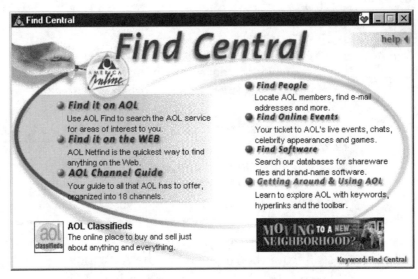

FIGURE 6.2: AOL's search HQ

TIP

When you get the list of results to your search, you can do a cursory screen of each area by double-clicking its name to go there and then using the Find in Top Window command (Edit ➤ Find in Top Window or Ctrl+F) to see whether the item or text you want is readily accessible.

The AOL Find features in Find Central are quite easy to use, so I won't bore you with unnecessary detail. A few highlights, though, are in order:

 You can not only search for people with Find People, you can search for your soul mate through a link to AOL's personals.

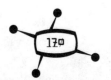

 Under Find Online Events, you can search for special events and weekly schedules in the chat and conference rooms. There's also a What's Hot link here. Note that you can also search chat rooms via the toolbar's Find ➤ Chat.

 Find Software! My favorite. Besides the usual, you can check out the daily download item, which is a random shareware executable of some type or another. Useful, silly, what's the diff? Check it out!

 Getting Around AOL sends you right to the Member Services Online Help files, if that's what floats your boat.

 The insidiously inviting AOL Classifieds square deserves mention. So I've mentioned it. (See Chapter 7 for a thorough discussion of the AOL classifieds.)

NOTE

There are other ways to browse, floating soft as a cloud through the myriad areas of AOL. I introduce you to the ways and means later in the chapter, under *Browsing Left Field*.

THE INTERNET SEARCH ENGINE FOR YOU

There are several different types of search engines out there; some search the Web and Usenet newsgroups, some just the Web, some search even more narrowly, well-filtered Web sites—

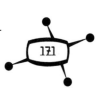

the G-rated stuff. There are also sites specifically geared toward searching for e-mail addresses of people and businesses.

NOTE

Though the Web is the most heavily used part of the Internet, it is by no means the whole thing. I discuss searching other parts later in this chapter under *Run with the Wolves, Burrow with the Gophers*.

In addition to search engines, there are metasearch sites, which house many search engines on one site. Some even allow you to access more than one engine to perform your search.

WARNING

I need to mention the obligatory caveat: While all the files available for downloading on AOL—including those uploaded by AOL members—are checked for viruses and functionality, everything else is fair game for yucky stuff. Be very careful when downloading a file from a Web site or Usenet newsgroup.

WEB AND USENET SEARCHES

These search engines automatically search both the World Wide Web and Usenet newsgroups for links to your topic.

AOL NETFIND

Internet ➤ AOL NetFind
`http://www.aol.com/netfind/`
Default is Boolean OR

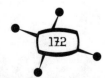

 With AOL's NetFind you can search the Web, search for a person, search for a business, and search newsgroups. Built on Excite's search engine capabilities, AOL NetFind searches not only for the search words you type in, but also for words closely related to your search words. So if you type in **custodian**, AOL NetFind will also look for items about janitors and sanitation engineers.

Wildcards and Other Operators

+   requires following search word to appear in each search result

-     requires following search word to be absent in each search result

""   place around any number of words you want searched for as a phrase

Boolean Operators

AND   search will reveal only profiles containing both words

OR   search will reveal profiles with either word

NOT   that word will not appear in the search results

( )   group words together so you can search for a couple of different options at a time

AltaVista

http://www.altavista.digital.com
Default is Boolean OR

 AltaVista recognizes a broad range of wildcards and Boolean operators. If you're going to search with this engine, be sure to use them; AltaVista is very powerful and can be overwhelming when not harnessed properly.

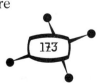

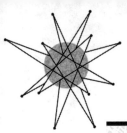

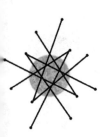

A Note about Boolean Operators

Whatever kind of Internet search you do, Boolean and other operators are your friends. Operators (words, wildcards, and other symbols) act like mathematical symbols; they tell the search engine what search words to link how. Using operators is kind of like mini-programming, if you can stand the cool-nerd aura of it.

Some search engines don't recognize all of the operators, and I carefully specify which operators work with which search engine. When using Boolean operators, uppercase them and be sure to include a space before and after each one.

I also indicate in each description what the Boolean default of each search engine is: AND or OR. A search engine that defaults to Boolean OR will, when looking for a phrase, return sites with *any* of the words, not necessarily the whole phrase. Dragsters, right?! A default to Boolean AND will return only sites containing *all* the specified search words—which is more like it.

In addition, you should know that searches are case-sensitive. As an added bonus, the Advanced Query page allows you to weight keywords.

Wildcards and Other Operators

* *   substitutes for any string of characters

* ?   substitutes for one letter

* -   requires following search word to be absent in each search result

* ""   place around any number of words you want searched for as a phrase

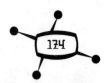

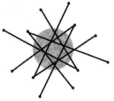

Boolean Operators

AND   search will reveal only profiles containing both words

OR   search will reveal profiles with either word

AND NOT   that word will not appear in the search results

NEAR   results will have the linked words within 10 words of each other

( )   group words together so you can search for a couple of different options at a time

Excite

http://www.excite.com
Default is Boolean OR

Much like AltaVista, Excite supports high-tech search strings (however, its Power Search is graphical only). Stuff you oughta know: two capitalized words next to each other are treated like a proper name, so if you wish to search for a proper name plus another word ("Bill Clinton" AND veto), put the name in quotes.

Wildcards and Other Operators

*   substitutes for any string of characters

\+   requires following search word to appear in each search result

\-   requires following search word to be absent in each search result

""   place around any number of words you want searched for as a phrase

Boolean Operators

AND   search will reveal only profiles containing both words

OR   search will reveal profiles with either word

AND NOT that word will not appear in the search results

( )   group words together so you can search for a couple of different options at a time

HotBot

http://www.hotbot.com
No Boolean default

   If you resist the cool geekiness that glows around every Boolean-expression user, HotBot is the site for you. It uses a graphical interface that gives you the same options as Boolean operators would—without the telltale glow.

Another advantage to HotBot is that you can search for files by their file type (Adobe Acrobat, Java, and so on). If you choose to do so, you'll want to search one file type at a time. In addition, you can save your Expert section settings for future use. The downside to HotBot is that it doesn't recognize wildcards, nor does it automatically look for plurals; thus you will want to link the singular and plural of your important search words with OR to make sure you get all the pertinent results.

Infoseek

http://www.infoseek.com
Default is Boolean AND

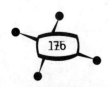

 **infoseek**™ In addition to the below functionality, be aware that two capitalized words next to each other are treated like a proper name. Also, if you want to search for several proper names, separate them with commas. When you find a site that gives you what you need, use the Similar Pages link for more excellent results.

Wildcards and Other Operators

*	substitutes for any string of characters
+	requires following search word to appear in each search result
-	requires following search word to be absent in each search result
|	narrow by placing between a broad-category search word and a narrow-category search word (cat | Manx)
""	place around any number of words you want searched for as a case-sensitive phrase
-	place between words you want adjacent to each other (non-case-sensitive)
url:	search for links to a URL
site:	search for pages at a particular Web site
{}	search words in brackets will appear within 100 words of one another

WEB-ONLY SEARCHES

Though some of the following search engines sport links to search engines that service other areas of the Internet, they are Web-only search engines at heart.

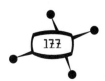

Lycos

http://www.lycos.com
Default is Boolean OR

Lycos is another search engine where the graphical interface—including a Power Panel allowing you to customize your search—can substitute for Boolean operators. It does, however, recognize the following wildcards and operators.

Wildcards and Other Operators

+	requires following search word to appear in each search result
-	requires following search word to be absent in each search result
""	place around any number of words you want searched for as a phrase

Boolean Operators

AND	search will reveal only profiles containing both words
OR	search will reveal profiles with either word
NOT	that word will not appear in the search results
ADJ	the words will appear next to each other
NEAR	the linked words will appear within 25 words of one another
FAR	the linked words appear more than 25 words apart at least once in result

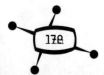

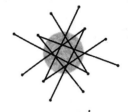

BEFORE   words appear in specified order but not necessarily near each other

O   directly before another operator (OADJ) will force results to be in order you specify

/#   use directly after ADJ, NEAR, and FAR to specify the # of words allowed between search words

Open Text Index

http://index.opentext.net
Default is Boolean AND

Not only does Open Text Index operate from a graphical interface, it's also case insensitive (it's nice to give those pinkies a rest from time to time). Open Text Index doesn't automatically search for plurals of your search words, so be sure to link the singular and plural of each search word with OR.

However, you can use your hard-won understanding of Boolean operators by doing a PowerSearch; here you can choose the following operators from a drop-down list.

Boolean Operators

AND   search will reveal only profiles containing both words

OR   search will reveal profiles with either word

BUT NOT   that word will not appear in the search results

NEAR   results will have the linked words within 80 words of each other

FOLLOWED BY   results will have the linked words within 80 words of each other in the order you type in

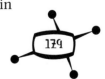

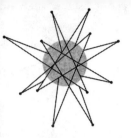

WEBCRAWLER

http://www.webcrawler.com
Default is Boolean OR

Wildcards and Other Operators

""   Put quotes around any number of words you want searched for as a phrase

Boolean Operators

AND   search will reveal only profiles containing both words

OR   search will reveal profiles with either word

NOT   that word will not appear in the search results

NEAR/#   results will have the linked words within the specified number (#) of words of each other

ADJ   results will have linked search words adjacent to and in order of words you type in

( )   group words together so you can search for a couple of different options at a time

SEARCHING FILTERED WEB CONTENT

You can feel safe using these search engines; the search engine elves have scrutinized the content of these sites to make sure they're as pure as the driven snow.

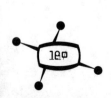

Magellan

http://www.mckinley.com/
Default is Boolean OR

Searching with this engine's Reviewed Sites Only and Green Light Sites Only options turns up only the best in Web sites.

Wildcards and Other Operators

+	requires following search word to appear in each search result
-	requires following search word to be absent in each search result
""	place around any number of words you want searched for as a phrase

Boolean Operators

AND	search will reveal only profiles containing both words
OR	search will reveal profiles with either word
AND NOT	that word will not appear in the search results
( )	group words together so you can search for a couple of different options at a time

Yahoo

http://www.yahoo.com
Default is Boolean AND

 Another search engine in the graphical-interface category, Yahoo allows you to narrow your search through its advanced graphical search format. To get to the advanced search, click the Options button. One thing to keep in mind is that Yahoo's default is to place a wildcard after every search word. Yahoo does recognize the following operators:

Wildcards and Other Operators

*	substitutes for any string of characters
+	requires following search word to appear in each search result
-	requires following search word to be absent in each search result
""	place around any number of words you want searched for as a phrase
t:	search word will appear in title
u:	search word will appear in URL

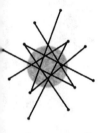

USENET SEARCHES

If you want solid newsgroup searching and don't care one whit about the Web, you have a few good options.

AOL NetFind Newsgroup Finder

Internet ➤ Search Newsgroups
`http://www.aol.com/netfind/newsgroups.html`
Default is Boolean OR

Discussed in more detail under *Web and Usenet Searches*, the newsgroups you'll find through AOL NetFind are rated according

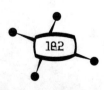

to how trafficked and informative they are, their technical level, and the rationality level of the newsgroup contributors.

REFERENCE.COM

`http://www.reference.com`
No Boolean default

This engine will search not only Usenet news-groups but also mailing lists and Web forums. (Web forums are message boards located at different Web sites all over the Internet.)

Boolean Operators

AND search will reveal only profiles containing both words

OR search will reveal profiles with either word

NOT that word will not appear in the search results

NEAR results will have the linked words within several words of each other

DEJANEWS

`http://www.dejanews.com/`
Default is Boolean AND

The source for Internet Discussion Groups, DejaNews has some spiffy search capabilities. Quite well-stocked in the operator arena, DejaNews also allows you to specify whether a search word is an

author, subject, newsgroup, or creation date. Thus, the search string **Dilbert ~a Adams** will find you Scott Adams' famous comic strip.

Wildcards and Other Operators

^	substitutes for any string of characters
?	substitutes for one letter
""	place around any number of words you want searched for as a phrase
{}	searches words alphabetically ranged between the two words enclosed by braces

Boolean Operators

AND	search will reveal only profiles containing both words
OR	search will reveal profiles with either word
AND NOT	that word will not appear in the search results
NEAR#	results will have the linked words within # words of each other
( )	group words together so you can search for a couple of different options at a time

Context Operators

~a	Author
~s	Subject
~g	Newsgroup
~dc	Creation date

METASEARCH SITES

The features available at metasearch sites vary widely: some are merely Web pages that link you to one site at a time; some actually perform concurrent searches on many different search engines' indexes. Below I list the search engines featured at each site and the things that'll help you decide whether or not a site is for you.

ALL4ONE

http://www.all4one.com

AltaVista	Lycos
WebCrawler	Excite

At All4One, you type in your search string once and see your search results in the four search engines' text boxes. Boolean expressions are recognized by the search engines that normally recognize 'em.

Highway 61

http://www.highway61.com

Excite	AltaVista
WebCrawler	Infoseek
Lycos	Yahoo

This site is hip. You can tell Highway 61 how patient you're feeling (this'll get stored as a cookie so the next time you search, the Highway will remember your tolerance level) and predict the highway-crossing skills of the armadillo. Oh yeah, and get results.

Inso

`http://wizard.inso.com`

AltaVista	Excite
HotBot	Infoseek
Lycos	Magellan
Open Text	WebCrawler
DejaNews (Usenet only)	

Inso is a Web site that houses several search engines but doesn't integrate them. Thus you can search with one search engine at a time. However, it does help you out with advanced queries, so if your Boolean isn't so hot, you might try it.

MetaCrawler

`http://www.metacrawler.com`

Excite	Lycos
Infoseek	Yahoo!
Open Text	WebCrawler
and others…	

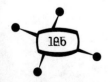

MetaCrawler recognizes Booleans AND, OR, and NEAR (yay!) and searches with all search engines at once, showing you the results on one page (and attributing each result to the search engine from whence it came). In addition, MetaCrawler features both MiniCrawler, an advertisement-free version of itself, and Power Search, which allows you to fine-tune your search-result screen.

ProFusion

http://www.designlab.ukans.edu/profusion/

AltaVista	Excite
HotBot	Infoseek
OpenText	Lycos
WebCrawler	Magellan
Yahoo	

I like this metasearcher because you can specify that it search with the three fastest engines, the three best, all, or only the ones you pick. Moreover, it tells you which engines support Boolean operators.

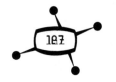

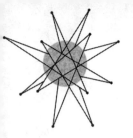

SavvySearch

`http://guaraldi.cs.colostate.edu:2000/form`

Yahoo	Excite
WebCrawler	Infoseek
DejaNews	Galaxy
Lycos	Magellan
Shareware.com	PointSearch
LinkStar	And more…

A simple interface allows you to search a bunch of search engine indexes at once. Only the search engines that've produced good results to searches like yours are invoked to get you your results, but you can specifically include all or any of the search engines in your search.

Yahoo's All-in-One Search Pages

`http://www.yahoo.com/Computers_and_Internet/Internet/`
`World_Wide_Web/Searching_the_Web/All_in_One_Search_Pages/`

If none of the other search engines and metasearch sites I've mentioned are doin' it for ya, try Yahoo's list of search pages.

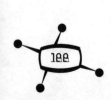

From the goofily named—Coolnerds Mega-Search, Dogpile, Fly-catcher—to the serious—like the Ultimate Search Page—Yahoo's page links you there.

Finding People and Businesses

If you're looking for an old buddy or a potential employer, you'll want to start off with a search engine geared specifically toward finding people and places. The search sites below have indexed a goodly amount of addresses, both e- and snail mail. Most of them require that you enter the last name of the person you're looking for, but some allow wildcards in case you're not certain of the spelling.

On AOL

Keyword **yellow pages** will take you to AOL's Switchboard, where you can perform a search for a person or business. Though the people-search options are few, the advanced option allows you to narrow the search by affiliation; from Cornell University alumni to affiliates of Ducks Unlimited, this site has 'em all.

Bigfoot

http://www.bigfoot.com

The advanced search option allows you to search Bigfoot's directory or the White Pages by name and state or e-mail address.

Four11

`http://www.four11.com`

This site has an excellent power search feature that allows you to type in old organizations or locations you have in common with your searchee, plus a Smart Name feature that searches for *Sue*, *Susan*, and *Susie*, even if only *Sue* is specified.

Internet Address Finder

`http://www.iaf.net`

Wildcards are allowed, but the scope of the search interface is rather limited.

WhoWhere

`http://www.whowhere.com`

WhoWhere has a couple of advanced search options to help you find that special someone's e-mail address or home phone and address.

Classmates

`http://www.classmates.com`

This site is specifically geared toward helping high school alumni find each other well into their golden years.

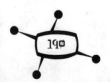

Masha Baitchauk's How to Find People's E-Mail Addresses Page

http://sunsite.oit.unc.edu/~masha/

This site has some suggestions for narrowing your search plus a slew of links to specialized search services. It's good lost-friend browsing for a rainy Saturday.

RUN WITH THE WOLVES, BURROW WITH THE GOPHERS

Gopher is not colorful, it isn't exciting, but it *is* extremely well organized and easy to find information on. Basically, Gopher is a hierarchical set of text links that allow you to tunnel deeper and deeper toward the object of your search by passing through logical and progressively narrower menu options.

Keyword **gopher** will take you to AOL's burrowing point, illustrated in Figure 6.3; from here you can browse neat-o Gopher sites, search Gopherspace with Veronica (like Jughead, one of Gopher's search engines), or browse through the world's Gopher sites. If you need to do some serious research, don't overlook Gopher.

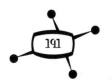

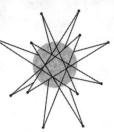

FIGURE 6.3: Dig, little gopher, dig!

NOTE

There are other searchable areas of the Internet, such as Telnet and WAIS; to learn more about searching these, check out Christian Crumlish's *Internet: No Experience Required* (Sybex, 1997). I touch on FTP, yet another searchable area of the Internet, in Chapter 1, *Excelling in E-Mail*.

BROWSING LEFT FIELD

Sometimes you just want to find something—you don't care what, it just has to be interesting. Start off by going to keyword

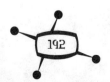

random; this keyword will send you to whatever AOL area it picks out of a hat. The first time I browsed with Random, I went *way* left field to Dégriftour: Le Voyage à Prix Dégriffé.

If you want something in the infield, try keyword **keyword**. Here you can browse the currently definitive and up-to-date list of AOL keywords. Just like on the Internet, AOL areas come and go, so you'll want to check back here for new developments once in a while.

Another browsy thing to do if you're the festive type is to try typing in a current holiday or event as your keyword. A Halloween area often springs up in October, an Olympics area during the Olympics season, and so on.

For that just-sit-back-and-relax feeling, try exploring AOL and the Internet on a road trip. Keyword **road trip** will get you to your starting point (Figure 6.4), where you can review the scheduled road trips, sign up for as many as you like, or even volunteer to lead one. These trips go where the trip leader wants to take you, so buckle up and enjoy the ride!

FIGURE 6.4: The '60s meet the Jetsons here at hitchhiker central.

The International Channel also runs its own road trips, which are a must if you're curious about other cultures. You can visit Norway or learn about how others around the world celebrate the end-of-year holidays… whatever the international guides are up for, you can join in on. The International Road Trip Schedule is accessible from the bottom of the AOL Road Trip schedule.

And last but not least, take a half day to make yourself some cocoa and meander through Find ➤ AOL Channel Guide for a detailed index to AOL's Channel contents.

Rock the Favorite Place List

I won't bore you with URLs to my favorite online comics, bike magazines, and whatnot; instead, I've compiled useful sites that you can search to find stuff you want to find. I do bore you with my favorite hotlinks on my Website. Get there by visiting the Sybex website at http://www.sybex.com and looking up *America Online Amazing Secrets* in the catalog.

Humor

http://www.humorsearch.com/

Search the Web for humor sites. Yippee!

Maps

http://www.mapquest.com

I love this site. Here you can enter any US street address and get a detailed map of the area—a boon if you don't like asking for directions from gas station attendants.

MedAccess On-Line

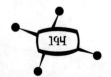

http://www.medaccess.com

Do you hate going to the doctor? Or just hate being uninformed about your ailments? Then this site is for you. Look anything up, from a doctor you're thinking of going to, to your diagnosis.

City.net

http://city.net

City.net is great if you're planning a trip. Here you can get info on any city anywhere anytime.

US Dept of Energy Computer Incident Advisory Capability

http://ciac.llnl.gov/ciac/CIACHome.html

Find the latest on computer viruses and Internet hoaxes on this very serious site.

Amazon Books

http://www.amazon.com

Amazon has a lot of books; new books, old books, rare out-of-print books. Order through their secure server or call with your credit card number; once you set your password, you can come back and order books on that same credit card time and time again.

Get a Job

http://www.getajob.com

Search for jobs by category, company, or region, check out the library of hints for getting and keeping a job, decide whether you're an eagle or a chicken... it's all along the way to Getting a Life!

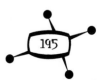

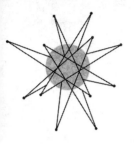

The Monster Board

http://www.monster.com/

A monstrous number of job listings as well as resume building tips and employer profiles await you at this site.

Auto-by-Tel

http://www.autobytel.com

Look for a new, previously owned, or leasable car through Auto-by-Tel. You'll be referred to the nearest dealership that houses their trained sales personnel, who will quote you a price that's close to cost without you having to haggle for it.

Consumer Reports

Keyword: **consumer reports**

Do a little research on the merchandise you plan to buy; make sure you know what to look for, get some hints on where to get it, and keep up with the latest recalls.

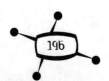

AOL's Today's News Channel

Keyword **news** ➤ Search & Explore

Browse the AOL News departments, get the best of the news, or customize a personalized to-your-mailbox news service.

THE WELCOME WINDOW SECRET

So you know that AOL logo in the Welcome window?

Have you ever passed your cursor over it? Notice how it turns into a pointing hand when you do that? Try clicking; you've found one of AOL's Easter eggs, a little hidden treasure of an area. This area changes every day.

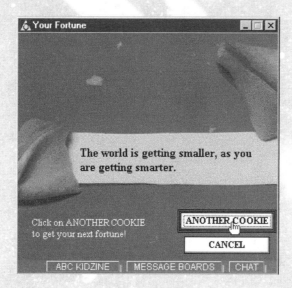

Chapter 7

Hunting for Bargains and Free Stuff

We all want to feel like we're getting the best deal on the products and services we buy—and if the provider offers it for free, all the better, right? Bargains, contests, and free stuff abound if you know where to look, both online and off. Offline you're on your own, but if you're after online bargains, you've come to the right place. In this chapter, I'll point you toward some good AOL and Web sites for getting your money's—or your talent's—worth.

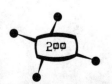

THE GOODS

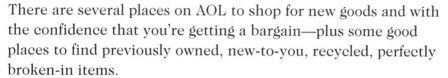

There are several places on AOL to shop for new goods and with the confidence that you're getting a bargain—plus some good places to find previously owned, new-to-you, recycled, perfectly broken-in items.

NOTE

Before you buy, ease your mind by checking out the AOL Guarantee, which you can find at keyword **guarantee**. AOL guarantees 100% purchasing satisfaction: AOL's merchants are certified by AOL (in addition to being stable businesses, AOL's merchants must agree to perform one-day order processing and e-mail turnaround as well as post complete customer service information and guarantees). In the event of credit card fraud (which is unlikely to happen), any damage is covered by AOL.

SHOPPER'S ADVANTAGE

Keyword **sa**

For an annual fee (at publication date, just $59.95), you too can be a Shopper's Advantage member, reaping such rewards as lowest-price guarantees on merchandise, an automatic 2-year warranty with everything you purchase through clubs, access to weekly specials, and SA's top deals on quality brand-name merchandise. At SA you can search for a specific item or browse the selections. My browsing turned up the impressive offer of 12 rolls of 24 exposure Kodak film at $28.60 to members, $50.10 to nonmembers.

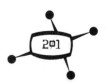

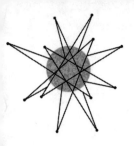

Magazine Outlet

Keyword **magazine outlet**

If clicking through online magazines doesn't cut it for you and you long for the days of curling up in your easy chair with Bubbles the cat warming your lap and a good zine to leaf through, Magazine Outlet guarantees the lowest prices on hundreds of magazine subscriptions.

For instance, you can save 80% off *Time*'s cover price (currently 52 issues for $30, compared to the regular subscription rate of $59.94). You can subscribe to 12 issues of *Wired* for $20 (compared to $39.95). And *American Woodworker* clocks in at 14 issues for $48. AOL's always adding magazines, so browse through once in a while to see what your current options are.

NOTE

Take these figures for what they are; impressive comparisons rather than hard fact. Prices change faster than books can be printed....

AOL Classifieds

Keyword **classifieds**

Dance with the wheelers and dealers at AOL Classifieds. Here you can post free or paid ads and browse the same for whatever post-pristine merchandise your heart desires (except for children to adopt, tobacco, firearms, alcohol, and explosives).

The difference between the free and the paid ads is that the free ads are posted on a bulletin board that's hidden a bit (and features bulletin board search capabilities only), and the paid ads are immediately accessible and searchable by region, category, or keyword.

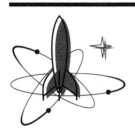

TIP

There are a *lot* more listings in the bulletin boards, so it behooves the smart shopper to check both places. Given this fact, the paid ads, though reasonably priced, are probably not a necessary use of your money.

To get to the bulletin boards:

1. Go to keyword **classifieds** (Figure 7.1).

FIGURE 7.1: Every community has its garage sales, flea markets, and thrift stores: AOL is no exception.

2. Click the Using AOL Classifieds icon. Using AOL Classifieds

3. Click Buy & Sell Bulletin Boards.
   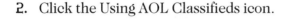 Buy & Sell Bulletin Boards

4. Choose your category. Once you get into the boards, the vehicles (for instance) are broken down by models and types. Though these aren't searchable geographically,

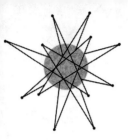

you can use the Find in Top Window command to narrow your search by model or year (as long as the advertiser put that information in the posting's subject line).

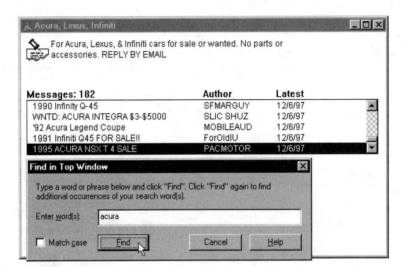

AOL Classifieds also offers you wiley traders a bulletin board, chat room, customer service, and trading guidelines.

WARNING

As with any sort of transaction, be very careful of cheats. AOL has written up some good guidelines that the smart seller and buyer will read and consider following. Find these guidelines in the Buyer/Seller folder of the Using AOL Classifieds area.

AOL Store

Keyword **aol store**

The AOL Store is like the campus store at your alma mater sans the candy counter and soda machine. Here you can buy toys, books, digital equipment, software, clothes....

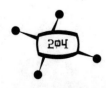

The prices are comparable to your campus store and other stores out there (like CompUSA), but it's definitely worth comparison shopping at the AOL Store. You might get lucky and hit a sale—and besides, where else can you buy an AOL varsity hooded sweatshirt?

THE SERVICES

Finding the right merchandise provider is just as important as finding the goods you need, but because the human element is inescapable, it's that much more challenging. Not only do you need to find *what* you want (for instance, a ticket from Boston to LA with a stopover in Quebec), but you need to find a provider that will procure it for you at the best price, preferably in a friendly and efficient way. You will find services of all kinds on AOL—after all, cyberspace is about providing information (I'm not going to touch the reliability issue here)—so what follows are just some highlights.

TIP

Even if you don't take advantage of the extended toolbar (discussed in Chapter 5), you can keep abreast of your AOL Perks at keyword **perks**. Special offers for AOL members include the AOL Visa, with which you can earn free AOL time, the sign-up-a-friend bonus ($20), AOL's long distance savings plan, and more.

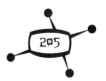

Traveler's Advantage

Keyword **ta**

For a yearly fee of (currently) $59.95, you get Traveler's Advantage's lowest-price guarantee (if you find a lower price on your fare, hotel, or car rental within 30 days of departure, TA will refund the difference); 5% cash back (this money usually becomes the travel agent's commission); special offers on hotels, cars, and plane fares; access to online booking arrangements; a tripfinder to help you decide on and organize your vacation itinerary; and 24-hour service.

If you travel frequently, you'll want to experiment with Traveler's Advantage (you can try it for 3 months for a buck).

Preview Travel

Keyword **preview travel**

Preview Travel (Figure 7.2) claims to be the most highly used travel service on AOL, and it's easy to see why. It keeps AOL members up to date on the latest airline, hotel, car rental, and other travel-related deals (such as the $88-$298 round-trip airfare American Airlines offered in late 1997), includes a News and Features section with weather advisories and travelers' journal entries, offers ready-made vacation packages for those of you who've planned one too many itineraries in your lifetime, plus gives you safety tips, emergency instructions, packing hints, and oh so much more.

Better yet for you infrequent travelers, there's no membership fee, though to get substantial information, you'll need to complete a brief travel profile.

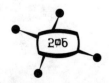

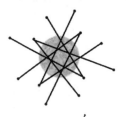

FIGURE 7.2: A travel service that almost makes it unaffordable to stay home!

AOL AutoVantage

Keyword **av**

If you're in the market for a new or used car, you can find out specs, experts' ratings, dealer and sticker prices, and past performance stats on the car of your dreams (or of your means).

If you want to take it further, you can fill out the Dealer Referral Form to get a quote on the car you're beginning to think of as yours. The quoted price is nonnegotiable, but it's quite fair as it's arrived at by adding a small profit (2-5%, a dealership profit approved by Consumer Reports) to the dealer's price.

If you want to take it still further, you would then visit the local dealership that provided the quote, test drive the car, and buy it (you can also finance the car through AutoVantage if you so choose). It sure beats playing the car salesman game.

AutoVantage also offers a club membership, which is somewhat like AAA and then some. For an annual fee of $79.95 (at the time of this writing) you get 24-hour roadside service, free service at select auto service centers, car buying assistance, car and hotel deals, maps, and trip planning.

Courses Online

Keyword **courses**

The Research & Learn channel brings you a way to attend adult-education classes at universities far and wide. In addition to the personal growth and enrichment offered at AOL's Online Campus, you can earn a certification or a graduate degree with University of California Extension classes and Phoenix University's programs.

AOL's Online Campus

This virtual college offers such diverse courses as Basic Conversational Navajo, Essential Spanish for Health Care Professionals, Math GED Preparation, Calculus I, Breadbaking, Starting a Successful Home Based Business, and Music Theory.

Courses are $25-50, depending on how long the course runs (most courses meet online once a week for 4 to 8 weeks). As with any school, getting to class (online fees) and materials are extra.

All AOL's Online Campus new courses are free the first time they're offered. There are not many in this category, but new courses are constantly being added. For my next career, I'm eyeing that Home Farmfishing for Profit class. At the very least I'll have a new hobby!

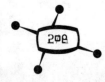

UC Extension Online

Select classes from the UC adult-education catalog (Figure 7.3) are offered online. You can find classes on quite a variety of subjects: C Language Programming, Intro to Human Physiology, Freshman Composition & Literature. To take a class, you enroll whenever the mood strikes you and then can take up to one year to complete the course.

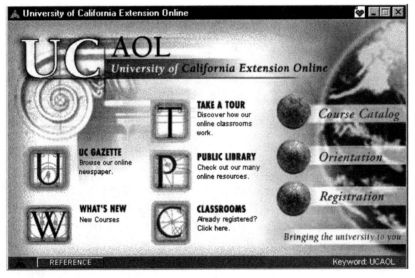
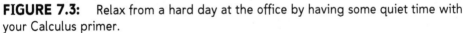

FIGURE 7.3: Relax from a hard day at the office by having some quiet time with your Calculus primer.

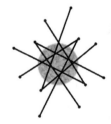

Course prices are comparable to UC Extension's real-world prices; Freshman Lit, for example, is $375 (textbooks extra).

UC Extension Online offers certificate programs in Hazardous Materials Management and Computer Information Systems Analysis and Design.

Phoenix U.

Phoenix University's online campus is geared toward allowing working adults to earn an undergrad or grad degree in their

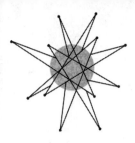

(your) spare time. Don't get too excited, though, unless you were planning on getting that degree in a business-related field.

Undergraduate degrees offered are BSs in Business Administration, Business Information Systems, Business Management. Graduate degrees you can earn are an MA in Organizational Management and MSs in Business Administration, Business Administration in Technology Management, Business Administration in Global Management, and Computer Information Systems.

Again, because the school is accredited, the cost is real-world; undergrad courses are $365 per credit, graduate courses $460 per credit.

THE MOTLEY FOOL SCHOOL

Keyword **motley fool**

Investing. It's what your parents are always urging you to do. If you feel at a loss when it comes to putting your money in someone else's hands, get the online investment skinny from the Motley Fool. Featuring advice on investing, and even on such satellite issues as buying a car and hunting for a job, the Motley Fool will gently guide you through the fine follies of money management in the most amusing way possible.

NOLO PRESS

Keyword **nolo**

The folks at Nolo really believe that, for most procedures, you can get by just fine without a lawyer. Their books and software steer you down the correct legal path without making you shell out more than the cost of said books, software, and whatever processing fees are necessary to get your case through the courts.

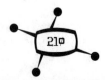

Nolo Press also has helpful books on other topics, such as buying a house or being a responsible landlady. Not only does Nolo's site have a helpful encyclopedia of legal topics, a tip of the day, and Shark Talk—a somewhat silly, rather bloody, but quite educational legal word game—it has an astounding collection of lawyer jokes.

Downtown AOL

Keyword downtown aol

AOL's Online Business Directory expands your list of goods and services to choose from by listing a large variety of businesses that have offices on the Web. You can browse the list or search it by business name or keyword.

Earning Cool Stuff

Winning stuff in contests adds an extra edge to the excellence of getting stuff free—not only was it free, you were smart enough to score it.

There are tons of contests in different areas all over AOL; your favorite areas and holiday areas might sponsor contests from time to time, so be sure to check those places in addition to the contests listed here.

Prizes range from the absurd to the sublime.

WARNING

Keep in mind that entering a contest means that you have consented, should you be a winner, to having your contest submission, name, and/or screen name used in promotions for the contest sponsor, AOL, and its affiliates. But who knows? It may be your 15 seconds of fame!

TRIVIA CONTESTS

These contests test your knowledge of the little (but terribly important) details of life (or flowers, or celebrities, or…). The way the contests usually work is that if you answer all (or a certain percent, depending on the contest) of the trivia questions correctly, yours are added to the pile of answers that are then subjected to a random drawing.

1–800–FLOWERS

Keyword **flowers**

1-800-Flowers sponsors a birthday trivia contest each month (winners net a $10 gift certificate for flowers).

CRUISE CRITIC

Keyword **cruise critic**

Answer trivia questions about (surprise!) cruises for a chance to win a cruise vacation. (Hint: you can find the answers by browsing the Cruise Critic area.)

ELECTRONIC GOURMET GUIDE

Keyword **gourmet guess**

This one's a food trivia contest; those foodies who score at least 7 of a possible 11 points go on to the random drawing stage. Prizes range from food posters to cutlery sets.

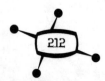

Moms Online

Keyword **moms online**

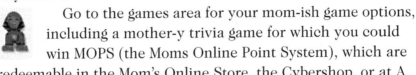

Go to the games area for your mom-ish game options, including a mother-y trivia game for which you could win MOPS (the Moms Online Point System), which are redeemable in the Mom's Online Store, the Cybershop, or at A Common Reader.

Talent Contests

If your thing is not little pockets of knowledge but a flourishing, as-yet-unrecognized talent, AOL's talent contests are for you. Ranging from creative writing to creative graffiti, AOL's contests are sure to include something that tugs at your special muse.

The Amazing Instant Novelist

Keyword **novel**

The Amazing Instant Novelist sponsors various writing contests that cover many topics, so if writing is your thing, look it up. You could win a resort vacation, a camera, and more cool shlag.

Antagonist Inc.

Keyword **ant**.

Here are the PC, Nintendo, and Playstation game contests—and there are many. The talent contest involves downloading the targeted game demo from the contest area and then rating it as creatively and accurately as you can. Tokens net you prizes like a weekend

in Washington, DC, Mechwarrior 2 game software, or a Jolt Cola Jockstrap!

Heckler's Online

Keyword **ho**

Do you have a sassy, insolent side to your creative patter? Heckler's Online has the contests for you! Pick from:

 Digital Graffiti: take the posted picture and apply your electronic spray paint.

 Daily Heckler's Gameroom chat room contests such as Altered States, where the gameroom hosts throw out the name of a state and you come up with as much interesting "information" about the state until the hosts call a halt to the frenzy. And then you do it again.

 Interactive Top Ten: HO provides the topic, you give one of the top 10 supporting statements. For example, one of the top 10 Disturbing Things to Read in Your Horoscope: *Signing an organ donor card today will save a life tomorrow* (courtesy of Mrs. Penny).

 Limerickization: write a limerick about the posted topic.

There are many more games at HO than I've listed, so let your mouse do the scurrying to find the perfect prize-winning competition for you. Winning in any of these nets you HO tokens, redeemable at the Prize Cellar. The prizes available in the Cellar span the gamut from Hog's Breath Hot Sauce to a Sony 27" TV.

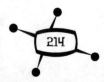

InToon

Keyword **intoon**

Click on Intoon with the News' Hot Air contest and fill in the cartoon balloon to fit (or not) the cartoon situation depicted. You could win a cartoon print—plus, of course, fame and recognition.

Moms Online

Keyword **moms online**

There are many venues for your motherly creativity at Moms Online. Click the Games icon for games, the Daily Sphinx for a daily vocabulary contest complete with silly story. The games section includes various chat and message board games such as serial story authoring, riddle solving, and anagram solving.

MOPS (Moms Online Point System) are redeemable in the Mom's Online Store, the Cybershop, or at A Common Reader.

Preview Travel

Keyword **vacations**

In the Preview Travel area, click on the Specials icon. Enter your best sob story (How badly *do* you need a vacation? Don't hold back, and you might win one!), travel photos (to win luggage), or travel tips (also to win luggage).

Urban Legends

Keyword **urban legends**

One month Urban Legends sponsored a UFO Stories contest, inviting you to share your wildest—and, of course, completely true—alien abduction story for Lost in Space paraphernalia. Check back for other contests.

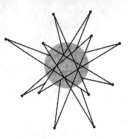

SCAVENGER HUNTS

Find it first and you win the prize! If you want to pit your keen instinct for scavenging and your mouse finger against other players, these are the contests you've been looking for.

Antagonist Inc

Keyword ant

Antagonist's scavenger contest involves scrutinizing the weekly demos for a riddle (tucked cleverly into any one of them) and then submitting your answer for the chance to win big. (These prizes include the Washington, DC/Jolt Cola Jockstrap range.)

Hub Music

Keyword hub musi

Hub Music's monthly contest involves collecting weekly clues and answering the monthly quiz questions correctly (based on the clues that have gone before) for a chance to win a $1,000 shopping spree at Tower Records.

RANDOM DRAWINGS

At this point you may be thinking, "To heck with the antics! I'm no circus elephant, standing on my head for the masses!" If you have no patience for showing off, but you just wanna win, try one of these random drawings.

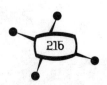

1-800-Flowers

Keyword flowers

You'll find a Birthday Bonanza at 1-800-Flowers, where you can enter a random drawing for a chance to win a birthday flower cake.

Antagonist Inc

Keyword ant

In the PC, Nintendo, and Playstation contests area you'll find some contests where all you gotta do is enter to (maybe) win cool Nintendo, Playstation, or PC games and stuff.

Housenet

Keyword housenet

Click the Rec Room icon to find the different random drawings this home-improvement site has to offer. Win a laser level that memorizes angles! Score architectural software with which to electronically daydream about your dream home!

Hub Music

Keyword hub music

The daily contest at Hub Music is a blind drawing for a CD or Tower Record t-shirts and other assorted crap.

Magazine Outlet

Keyword **magazine outlet**

This contest is a good example of what you can find if you keep tabs on your favorite areas; in December, Magazine Outlet had a sweepstakes where the grand prize was 1 million dollars.

Traveler's Advantage

Keyword **ta**

Traveler's Advantage has an annual Christmas sweepstakes, where visions of winning $25,000 in cash will dance with the sugar plums in your Christmas Eve head.

Getting It Free

And who can dispute the merits of finding free stuff? Cleaner (and less embarrassing) than dumpster diving, surfing AOL and the Web for free junk can be just as rewarding.

Many of the areas in AOL offer a free topic-specific newsletter, which is an excellent way to keep up with new things going on—chat schedules, hot games, whatever your interest is. And on the Internet, free stuff abounds. Below is a little list to whet your appetite; bone up on your searching skills (Chapter 6) and find your own little gems of price-less fun.

Games

Despite all the weird vibes you might get from the anthill talk at this site, you can still find some excellent demo software absolutely free at Antagonist inc. at keyword **ant**—Quake, Duke Nukem 3D, Tomb Raider 2, Andretti Racing, and more.

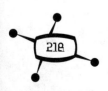

Virtual Flowers

Absolutely free, send your online sweetie a lovely picture of a flower arrangement at `http://www.virtualflowers.com/`.

Lotsa Free Stuff!

I'll leave you with a major find: WWW Virtual Sites at `http://www.dreamscape.com/frankvad/free.html` has links to gazillions of free things on the Web; cards, contests, screen savers, product samples, clip art, and tons more. Check it out, you'll be amazed.

Now that you've surrounded yourself with all the stuff money and talent can buy, let's give something back to the online world and create a Web site!

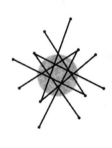

Chapter 8

Your Web Page

Okay, netizens! Whatever talent you have, it's time to shine it up and show it to the world! You may be an artist, writer, collector, or have some particular agenda to push; the Web's the place for you to show your stuff.

NOTE

Even if you don't have a particular purpose in mind, you can still create a Web page. However, to be blunt, I don't recommend it. You know Mirsky's Worst of the Web (recently reincarnated as Worst of the Web)? You don't want to end up there. So do yourself (and us innocent surfers) a favor and plan your site with care. Your fellow netizens will thank you.

As an AOL member, you are granted 2MB of Internet space per screen name absolutely free. I say *Internet* because you can

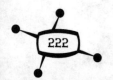

use these MBs by posting to your FTP folder or your Web site—or both. (For more information on your FTP site, see Chapter 1, *Excelling in E-Mail*.)

This chapter will concentrate primarily on the actual creation of your Web page: the how-to, the what-to-click, the where-to-go-for-art. I'll give you a few design pointers along the way, but there are some great books out there that will help you far more than will the few pages I can devote to the subject. The books I highly recommend are:

Effective Web Design: Master the Essentials (Navarro; Sybex, 1998)

Web Pages That Suck: Learn Good Design by Looking at Bad Design (Flanders and Willis; Sybex, 1998)

Web by Design: The Complete Guide (Holzschlag; Sybex, 1998)

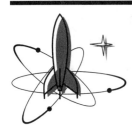

TIP

Don't forget that links to the Web sites mentioned throughout this book can be found on my Web site. Get there by going to http://www.sybex.com and looking up *America Online Amazing Secrets* in the Sybex catalog.

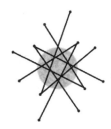

TIPS TO GET GOING WITH

Got your purpose? Got some ideas of how to make that purpose into a viable Web site plan? Good.

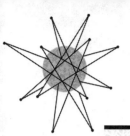

A Few Web Page Tips

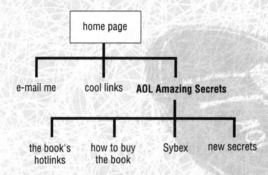

It can't hurt to sit down with some scratch paper and a scratcher and do a quick sketch of your proposed site: start with your home page at the top, and on the next line list the pages you want to link to, on the next line the pages you want those pages to link to, *DC al coda*, repeat, and so on. This way you'll get a good visual of the hierarchy you're proposing, you can make sure it'll make sense to the average surfer, and you can make sure you're planning something visually appealing that isn't too cluttered.

When thinking about what to put on your home page:

keep in mind that you want your home page to be interesting *and* quick to download (surfers won't wait long—think *seconds*—before giving up in disgust and moving on)

try to design each of your pages within a site in similar ways (just using the same background and text color will suffice) so visitors will feel confident that they're still with you

remember to include a statement of copyright on your page, unless you don't care whether your text and images appear elsewhere without being credited to you

include your e-mail address so people can contact you (for instance, to tell you if a link is broken on your site)

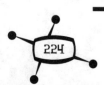

WARNING

Do *not* put your address or phone number on your Web site. If you want to name the general area you live in, that's okay. But the Internet is a big bulletin board for everyone to see, and you don't want to invite just anyone into your home.

Enough about *why* and *what*; on to *how*, *when*, and *where*.

NOTE

AOL's TOS agreement applies to your Web site, too.

AOLPRESS

Now for some fun!

AOLpress is a sophisticated tool for Web page creation and maintenance; it's not completely intuitive (which is where this chapter can help), but it's free and it's got a lot of excellent features. It gives you a great deal of versatility, so if you want anything resembling a professional look to your site, I recommend using AOLpress.

One of AOLpress' advantages is that you can create your Web site almost entirely offline (only popping online to find the URL of a link you want to create or to download a freeware graphic).

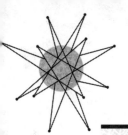

Personal Publisher

AOL's Personal Publisher, found at keyword **personal publisher**, is the ideal Web site tool for kids and adults not so keen on playing with software. It's super easy to create a simple page and super easy to post it to your personal Internet space (called *My Place*). Plus, Personal Publisher is a boon to those of you who are maxed out on hard drive space; everything is stored in AOL space (pages you're still working on are on AOL's home.aol.com server; pages you've uploaded to your Internet space are on AOL's members.aol.com server). On the downside, you need to be online to create and edit your page.

Personal Publisher is easy and unsophisticated enough that you won't have trouble using it to create a Web page; therefore, I won't go into the particulars. And, to be honest, I think AOLpress is by far the superior product; it looks more tech-y, but it's way more hands-on and visual.

Download FREE
AOLPress

Get the AOLpress software by going to keyword **aolpress** and clicking the Download FREE AOLpress icon on the right. It'll take a half hour or so, but it's well worth it. Once it's safely on your hard drive, navigate to the directory you downloaded it to and double-click the AOLpress executable file (mine was called *aolp2032.exe*; yours may be a more current version). You'll be guided through the installation process.

NOTE

You can use AOLpress to create a secure commercial Web site using PrimeHost; details are at keyword **primehost**.

CREATING YOUR HOME PAGE

AOLpress.exe

When you've got AOLpress installed, launch it by double-clicking the AOLpress.exe icon or by clicking Start ➤ Programs ➤ AOLpress ➤ AOLpress.

AOLpress will load with the Welcome to AOLpress window open. You can either explore the AOLpress tutorial and the documentation files, or you can go for it and open a blank page (File ➤ New ➤ New Page).

Let's start by creating a new page. Do the File ➤ New ➤ New Page thing, and then take a gander at Figure 8.1.

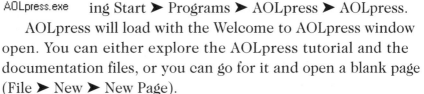

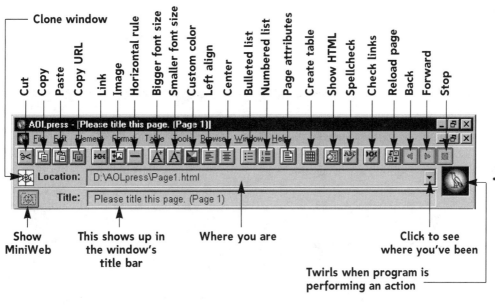

FIGURE 8.1: I heart toolbars.

You can begin typing your home page text now. You might want to say *Welcome!* Or create a heading alerting viewers to your site's purpose: *The Collectible Telephone.* Or start off with an image, which I'll get into later.

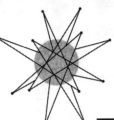

NOTE

At some point you'll want to replace the "Please title this page. (Page 1)" text in the Title field with what you want to show up in the title bar of your viewers' Web browser.

After you've typed in some text, you'll probably feel the urge to play with the look of the page; after all, black on grey is not that stimulating. To modify your page's look, click the Page Attributes button in the AOLpress toolbar. The Page Attributes dialog box, shown in Figure 8.2, will appear.

Pick your background color—or customize a color—from a color chart

Notify viewers of recent changes to your site

Browse your hard drive, disk, or an online site for a background image

Choose the color your regular paragraph text will be

Color your links

Alert your visitors to links they've already followed

Add link icons to your site that will allow visitors to easily move around your site

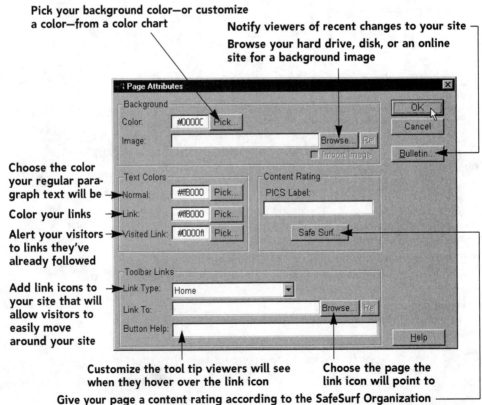

Customize the tool tip viewers will see when they hover over the link icon

Choose the page the link icon will point to

Give your page a content rating according to the SafeSurf Organization

FIGURE 8.2: Go wild—or don't.

NOTE

The SafeSurf Organization, which details its rating decisions at http://www.classify.org/safesurf/, was created by parents (big surprise) to allow families to make sound Web surfing decisions. To be honest, I don't think this rating is terribly useful, mostly because if you rate anything in the range of categories (from Glorifying Drug Use to Intolerance), it's got to be between *subtle innuendo* and *explicit and crude*. The system doesn't take into account 1. sites that don't touch on these subjects at all and 2. liars. Therefore, I recommend that you ignore this button and blow off rating your Web site altogether.

COLORS

Choose your colors by clicking the Pick button next to the item you wish to color (background or text) and choosing from the Color chart that pops up. If you're not happy with the colors provided, click the Define Custom Colors button at the bottom to open up the grand color square. From the expanded Color window, you can adjust color to the brilliance or sobriety you prefer, then add your new color to the Color palette.

Click around to create a custom color

Choose a color and click OK ▶

Your new colors will show up in these rows ▶

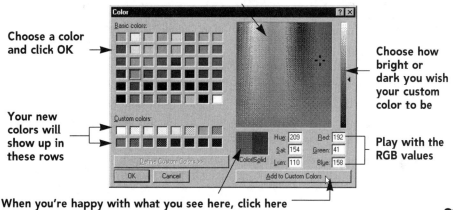

Choose how bright or dark you wish your custom color to be

Play with the RGB values

When you're happy with what you see here, click here ⸺

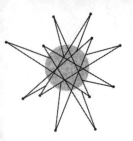

BACKGROUND IMAGES

Choose a background image from the Page Attributes dialog box by clicking the Browse button by the Background Image field. The Insert Image dialog box (Figure 8.3) gives you a lot of flexibility in choosing your image; you can navigate to an image on your hard drive and select that, you can pop in a CD or disk and select an image from that medium, or you can surf online to a place that offers uncopyrighted art for general use and select it.

WARNING

Be very careful when appropriating others' images for your own use. If the site is marked All Rights Reserved or uses other such uncompromising language, respect that and don't lift images or text from it. If the site asks that the owner be contacted for permission prior to use, respect that and send off an e-mail detailing exactly what you want to use, why, and how you plan to use it. This warning is not just to protect your karma; your pocketbook could be in jeopardy if you are caught stealing others' work and are sued.

Once you've found a satisfactory background image, click OK in the Insert Image dialog box. You'll see, back at the Page Attributes box, that the path for the file has been entered into the Image field.

Notice the Import Image check box directly under the Browse button? If you've meandered over to a CD or on the Web to gather your image, check this box to capture the image to your hard drive. It'll be saved to the directory you're in—for instance,

C:\AOLpress—as a GIF file. Now you won't need to worry about the Web site path being correct or the disk being in (which would be extremely inconvenient).

3. **Highlight the desired file**   **2.** **Navigate around your hard drive, disk, or site**

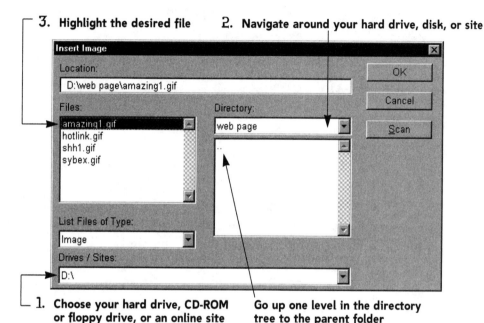

1. **Choose your hard drive, CD-ROM or floppy drive, or an online site**   **Go up one level in the directory tree to the parent folder**

FIGURE 8.3:   XBMs, JPEGs, and GIFs, oh my!

TIP

When you consider colors, images, and backgrounds, coordinate the seriousness or wackiness you create with what you want your viewers to get from your site. A site that uses a monochrome background (as in, all black) and tastefully placed images is a site that will be read for its content. A site that uses a wild background and lots o' art is a site that will be experienced primarily as a burst of color. People may read the content as well, but content will be experienced, even if subconsciously, as secondary.

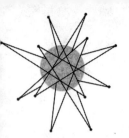

You can fiddle with the text using the size and alignment toolbar buttons, or get fancy with the options under Format on AOLpress' menu bar. These options include anything from bold-face to different heading styles to alignment, and they're self-explanatory, so experiment.

TIP

To make sure returns between paragraphs show up, use a forced line break (Element ➤ Forced Line Break or Shift+Return).

Back at your page, if you only see a portion of your background image, it's because 1. It's huge and 2. You don't have text filling in the foreground for there to be a background for. In other words, if you type a few paragraphs (or just press Enter a bunch of times), you'll scroll down your page and the rest of your background graphic will appear.

Statement of Copyright

Before we move on to adding images, I'll finish the home page litany by urging you again to place a copyright statement on your page. To do so:

1. Type **Copyright** *YourName TheYear* at the bottom of the page.

2. In the AOLpress toolbar, choose Tools ➤ Show HTML.

3. Place your cursor after the word *copyright* and type:

    a space

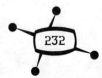

©

another space

4. The HTML code should look like this (for instance):

`Copyright &copy; Laura Arendal 1998`

5. Click the Close button in the upper-right corner and Apply in the confirmation dialog box; you should now see a copyright symbol between the word *copyright* and your name.

Copyright © <u>Laura Arendal</u> 1998

NOTE

To invite e-mail from your visitors, select the text (such as your name) that will clue them in to the ability to send you mail and, from the AOLpress menu bar, choose Element ➤ E-Mail Link. In the E-Mail Link box, type in your e-mail address and click OK.

ADDING IMAGES

Art, though sometimes an effort to download, is fun. Images can be merely decorative, or you can use images—such as photos—to open up new worlds to your visitors. Images can be the self-created kind, whether just in Paint, or in a professional program like CorelDRAW, or by hand and scanned; they can be photos (also scanned); and they can be Clip Art you've purchased or found on a Web site amenable to sharing such things.

Later in this chapter I go into where to get clip art and software for art creation, so for now let's just run through how to add an image to your page.

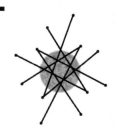

To include an image on your Web page, either choose Element ➤ Image or click the Image icon in AOLpress' toolbar. You'll get an Image dialog box, as shown in Figure 8.4.

FIGURE 8.4:   Add yer frills and doodads here.

As you did when you chose your page's background image, click Browse to get to the Insert Image dialog box (shown back in Figure 8.3), navigate to the image's location, select it, and click OK to get back to the Image dialog box.

Now that you've selected your image, you can modify a few things about its appearance.

Alignment is easy; the trick here is that if you want to have your image appear beside text, rather than over or under it, you'll want to choose Floating's Left or Right option.

The **Dimensions** boxes allow you to size your image up or down. Unless you have specific dimensions in mind, it's easier to OK the image and, on the Web page, double-click it to show a dotted border and sizing handles. Drag'n'drop with the sizing handles until you're pleased with the image's size.

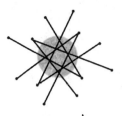

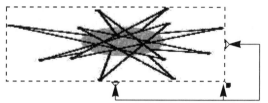

Sizing handles

The **Display Description** field allows you to type in descriptive words that will show up when a visitor hovers the cursor over this image. It's also a tip of the hat to those who are surfing with Web browsers that don't, for some reason, show graphics—not to mention the possibilty of something happening to your image link so that visitors see a broken image graphic instead of your beautiful piece; at least, in the above situations, visitors will know what they're missing.

NOTE

That said, I think image descriptions are a bit annoying. If you decide to create a link from an image or an Image Map, where certain areas of an image link to different pages (described later in this chapter), the image description can become confusing as it only describes the image, not the link(s) it points to.

Show Link Border alerts visitors to the fact that the image is indeed a link by showing a border around the image in your link and visited-link colors.

When you're happy, click OK. If you ever want to change something about the image, just select it and click the Image button to get back to this dialog box.

Absolute and Relative Links

Now for some logistics. You'll notice in the Image dialog box in Figure 8.4 that there, beside the Browse button, is a button called *Abs*. This stands for *Absolute*, and it describes the type of pathway stored in the location box. Furthermore, this button is toggle-able; pathways can be Absolute or Relative. The difference is important and will inform how you create and maintain your Web site.

An **Absolute** pathway is a complete pathway that contains in its location information the exact path anyone would take to get to the file or image you're showing. In other words, if you insert an image from another Web site and wish to retain the Web site pathway (perhaps the Webmaster changes the image regularly and you want your site to stay current), you would keep the original Web site's URL in the Location field (for instance, http:// www.sybex.com) and you would retain its Absolute standing.

A **Relative** pathway is one that is only relevant from the page you're on. For instance, if you're already on my Web site and you link to another page that's on my site, you'll be following a Relative reference. The Location field in this case might read /CoolLinks.html (rather than http:// www.sybex.com/CoolLinks.html, its Absolute counterpart).

NOTE

The challenge here is that what you see on the button is opposite of what the link is; this way, if your link is Absolute and you want to make it Relative, you'll be seeing the Rel button and thus be able to click it to change the link's type. But it sure looks odd!

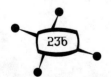

Image Mapping

Image mapping is cool. Got an image on your page? Does this image consist of many smaller images that could refer to many links? If so, then you have a good image with which to create an image map. You can make an image map out of any picture, but you want to be sure the references within it are clear to your visitors (otherwise, what's the point?).

For instance, take my Web site. I've created an image map using art from this book; The image's main purpose is to take you right to the page I've created to give you more information about this book, but if you move your cursor around the image, you'll see that I've connected several of the words to other web sites.

To create your image map:

1. Select your image on your AOLpress page, then choose Element ➤ Image Map.

2. The AOLpress Image Map window will blossom as shown in Figure 8.5; here is where you divide and link your image.

3. Select a shape from the Image Map toolbar.

4. Drag the cursor over the area you wish to enclose with this shape.

5. Select the Arrow tool and click the shape you just drew to select it; now you can move it by dragging and dropping, and size it via the sizing arrows.

6. When you're a-okay with the shape's placement, head to the Location field and either type in the pathway you want this area of your image to link to, or click the Browse button to navigate to the page of your linking desire.

Delete selected shape
Enclose the area you wish to link from
Select with the arrow
I have selected this shape; its link shows up in the Location field
I'm hovering over this shape; its link shows up as a tool tip

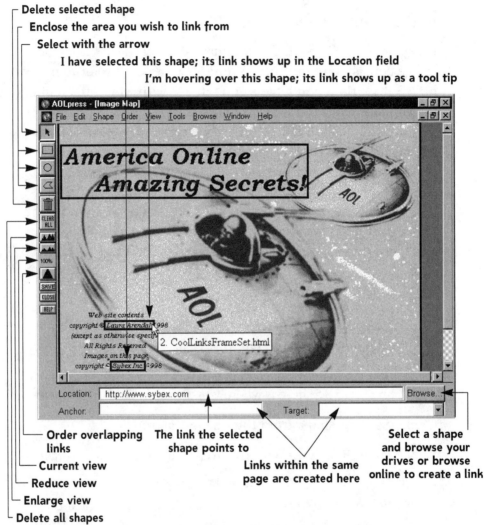

Order overlapping links
Current view
Reduce view
Enlarge view
Delete all shapes

The link the selected shape points to

Links within the same page are created here

Select a shape and browse your drives or browse online to create a link

FIGURE 8.5: An already-mapped page

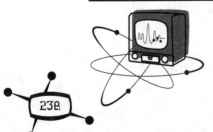

SECRET

For more control when moving shapes within the image map, use your keyboard's arrow keys to move the selected shape around.

7. When you've got the URL in your sights, click OK.

8. Repeat the above steps for each section of the image you want to link to another page.

If you decide you don't like a shape, select it and click the trash can icon to delete it. If you want to start all over with the same image, just click the Clear All button to delete all the shapes.

If any of your shapes overlap, you'll want to make sure that the frontmost shape is the one you want to be on top; the default will be whichever shape was drawn last, but that may not be what you want. An example of this situation can be seen on my page; I've made the entire image a link to the America Online Amazing Secrets page, and all the other shapes are placed on top of that square.

To order overlapping shapes:

1. Select the shape you wish to order.

2. Click the Order icon (it depicts a pyramid shape).

3. Make your choice:

 Bring Forward or Send Backward if there are three or more shapes overlapping and you wish this one to be the middle layer.

 Bring to Front if you want this shape to be the foremost link.

 Send to Back if you want this shape to be overshadowed by the other(s).

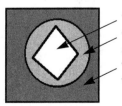

This shape must be in front; all of its area will be clickable

This shape must be in the middle; only the lightly shaded area will link to the correct location

This shape must be in back; only the heavily shaded area will link to the correct location

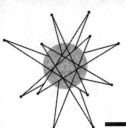

TIP

If you can't remember exactly how to edit something you've created on a page (or say you've copied some HTML from another page and you're using AOLpress to edit this material but don't know exactly how), just click Element ➤ Get Attribute. The correct dialog box will open up, and you can edit away.

LINKING TO OTHER PAGES

Now that you've done your text and images to a T, it's time to create links to other pages. If you haven't created other Web pages yet, feel free to do so now, or use the following instructions to create a link to a Web site you like.

You can create links with text and with images. It's easier for visitors to tell when text is a link; hotlinks are always underlined, and you can choose to make them a different color from the rest of your text (discussed earlier in this chapter). But it's fun to use images as links.

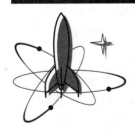

TIP

One time-honored image-link technique is to provide a thumbprint of a photo or picture, and encourage visitors to click the thumbprint to connect to a page showing the full-size picture. This technique saves wear and tear on visitors' patience; they can choose which big graphics to view, and it allows you to create a catalog of selectable, delectable images.

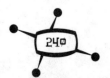

To create a link using text:

1. Highlight the words on your AOLpress page you want to become a hotlink.

2. Choose Element ➤ Link from the AOLpress menubar or the Link button from the toolbar.

3. In the Link dialog box that appears, either type in the URL you wish to become the link's destination, or click the Browse button and go find it.

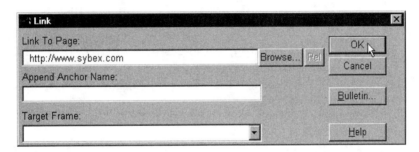

4. The selected text will now be underscored and in a different color (if you indeed chose to make your linking text a different color).

America Online Amazing Secrets is published by Sybex, an independent computer-book publisher in Alameda, California.

That's it! If you want to unlink text from its location, select the hotlinked text, then choose Element ➤ Unlink. If you want to change the link, select the text, click the Link button in the toolbar, and edit away in the Link dialog box.

TIP

Press the Ctrl key when you want to select a hotlink for editing; this will prevent you from linking.

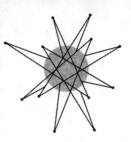

To create a link using an image, just select the image and follow the same steps as above. If you've enabled the Show Link Border option in the Image dialog box, your hotlinked image will now have a link-colored border around it. Otherwise, it will appear to be just an image, until some unwary visitor hovers her cursor over it and sees the linking page exposed in AOL's lower-left corner (muhahahaha!).

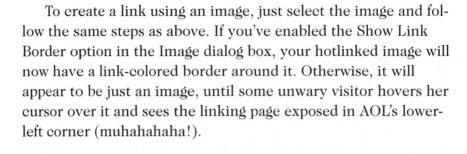

NOTE

If you use an image to create a hotlink, you might want to go back to the image description in the Image dialog box and type in the URL of the link, which is much more useful for most visitors than a mere image description.

Linking within a Page Using Anchors

Anchors are the devices by which you make links within a page. Using an anchor, you can, for instance, go from a heading on a page to the top of that page, or from the top of a page to a section several paragraphs down from the top. I use anchors on my America Online Amazing Secrets Links page, where at the top I've provided a table of chapter numbers, and below I've ordered the URLs discussed in the book by chapter. So if you want to see the URLs I discuss in Chapter 8, you'd click the 8 up at the top and be magically

Go to hotlinks from Chapter...

| 2 | 3 | 4 | 6 | 7 | 8 | 9 |

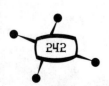

transported to the words *Chapter 8, Your Web Page*, which is the beginning of the URL listings for this chapter. Do you love it??

Chapter 8, *Your Web Page*
- Worst of the Web
- *Effective Web Design: Master the Essentials* (Navarro; Sybex, 1998)
- *Web Pages That Suck: Learn Good Design by Looking at Bad Design* (Flanders and Willis; Sybex, 1998)
- *Web by Design: The Complete Guide* (Holzschlag; Sybex, 1998)
- *Mastering Photoshop for the Web* (Straznitskas; Sybex, 1998)

THE LINKING TO AOL KEYWORDS SECRET

You can also create links to AOL keywords. However, you cannot follow these links with AOLpress. In fact, the only people who can follow these links are people who are accessing the Web with AOL's Web browser.

To link to an AOL area:

1. Determine the keyword for the area.

2. Select the linking text on your page.

3. Click the Link button in the AOLpress toolbar.

4. In the Link to Page field, type **aol://1722:*keyword***. For example, to link to AOL's AOLpress area, you'd type **aol://1722:aolpress**.

Even if the AOL area you're linking to has a space in its keyword, don't include a space when typing the keyword into the Link dialog box's Link to Page field. So, for instance, to provide a link to AOL's Personal Publisher, you'd type **aol://1722:personalpublisher**.

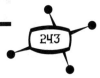

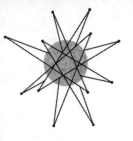

Here's how to create links within your Web page:

1. Place your cursor at the place you want to link to. This will be your anchor.

2. Choose Element ➤ Anchor and name your anchor. (This name will show up as a tool tip when a visitor hovers his mouse over the linking text.)

Chapter 9, *Accessing AOL at Home and On the Road*

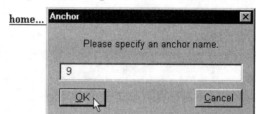

3. Click OK.

4. Now go find or create the text you wish to link to your anchor. Select the text or image you wish to become this link.

5. Choose Element ➤ Link or click the Element button in AOLpress' toolbar.

6. In the Append Anchor Name field, type the name of your anchor and click OK.

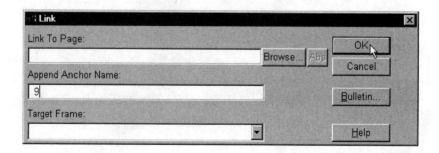

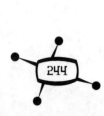

Try it! Click on the linking text; your browser should have whooshed you, smooth as a small creek iced over in the dead of winter, to your anchor text.

ADDING SOUND

You may want to add sound to your Web page (you've recorded your youngest jamming on the toy xylophone, or you've got a sound bite from your first garage band). You can always connect an external audio player (such as a cassette player) to your computer (via special cable) and record sounds into a software program; if you have a microphone and a sound card, you can record sounds directly into multimedia format. To check what audio applications you have at your disposal, click Start ➤ Programs ➤ Accessories ➤ Multimedia.

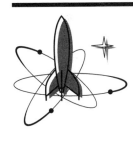

TIP

If you'd prefer to use already-created sounds, Lycos and Yahoo offer the ability to search specifically for sound files (though copyright considerations apply here, too!); you can also check out the Audio Browser Sound Files collection at http://www.webplaces.com/html/sounds/htm.

To create a link to your sound file:

1. Select the word(s) or image you want to become the link.

2. From AOLpress' menu bar, choose Element ➤ Link.

3. In the Link dialog box, click Browse.

4. In the File to Link To dialog box, choose Sound in the List Files of Type field on the lower left.

5. Navigate to your file, highlight it, and click OK.

6. Click OK in the Link dialog box.

Play it again, Sam!

NOTE

WAV files are the safest type of file to use on your Web page; most browsers recognize them, so your visitors should have little difficulty in your auditory garden of delights.

BACKGROUND SOUND

To add background sound to your page, you'll need to fool with the HTML coding a bit. Even if you don't relish the thought of looking at all that weird text, just follow along and your site will be hopping in no time. (I discuss HMTL a little more directly after this section.)

WARNING

Background sound files not only make your Web page take longer to download, they can also be embarrassing for those who are visiting from work. "Just taking my 15-minute break" only works so many times.

To include background sound at your site:

1. Open your Web page in AOLpress.

2. Choose Tools ➤ Show HTML.

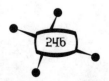

3. Place your cursor after the \<body> tag and press return to start a new line.

4. Type the following lines:

   \<embed src=*"filename*.wav" autostart="True" loop="True" hidden="True">

   \<bgsound src=*"filename*.wav" loop=infinite>

   Filename.wav is the name of the WAV file you want to run in the background.

NOTE

The \<embed> tag is recognized by Internet Explorer and Netscape Navigator, but relies on proper plug-ins to work. *Plug-ins*, which are additional pieces of software you can attach to your browser, can be downloaded from your browser's homepage. For IE, this page is http://www .microsoft.com. For Navigator, you'll want to go to http:// www.netscape.com. The \<bgsound> tag is recognized only by Internet Explorer (AOL's built-in browser), and should play without problems for fellow AOLies and other IE users. The \<bgsound> tag isn't recognized by AOLpress' parser, but don't worry about that.

5. Upload your WAV file to your My Place venue, using the FTP upload instructions back in Chapter 1.

After you save your page to your Web site, you can navigate to it using AOL's browser to hear the beautiful melodies you've thrown out to the world.

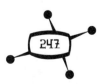

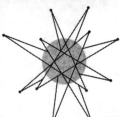

NOTE

Remember that AOLpress is not really a Web browser; it's a Web page tool. You won't be able to hear your sound files (nor watch your animated gif move around) from AOLpress.

FRAMES

Frames are groovy; frames add clutter. Frames are a way of dividing one screen into several different Web pages. They're groovy because you can have a lot of things going on at once; for instance, a hotlinked outline could appear in one frame, the text that the hotlinks link to in another, a third, related topic or image in yet another.... And that's also exactly why frames clutter up your Web page. They're groovy because they allow you to add to the information you present a level of clarity that wasn't there before. But more information also means... yes. More clutter.

WARNING

Not only are frames complicated to look at, they can be complicated (and frustrating) to navigate around, depending on what sort of Web browser your visitors are using. They're also not terribly easy to create. Still interested? Proceed with care.

Figure 8.6 gives you an idea of what I'm talking about here, in case you haven't run into frames before.

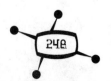

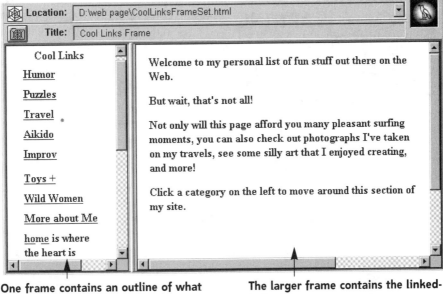

One frame contains an outline of what visitors can link to from this page

The larger frame contains the linked-to text

FIGURE 8.6: A good use of frames: an outline and informative text

The Truth about Frames

Before I get into how you can create a page with frames, let me expound on a little frame theory first (really, it's important). To do the frame thing, you need to create a special sort of page, called a FrameSet page. This page supports frames, while regular pages do not. The FrameSet page is what your less-optimally-browsered viewers will see.

The FrameSet page you create will automatically have a page-size frame in it; you can alter this frame, as I discuss below, to outfit your page with as many frames as you like. Certainly there's no point in creating a FrameSet page to just show the FrameSet page itself or just one frame page, so you'll want to adorn your page with a minimum of two frames.

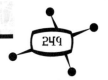

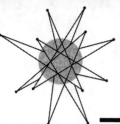

WARNING

Older Web browsers don't support frames, so anything you do with frames will have to be supplemented by text on the page the unfortunate users of old Web browsers will see. I'll describe what to do about this situation later.

Creating a Page with Frames

To create a FrameSet page with two frames:

1. From the AOLpress menu bar, choose File ➤ New ➤ New FrameSet. A FrameSet page sporting a shiny new frame appears.

2. To create a second, abutting frame, place your cursor over the edge of the window until a single-arrowed icon appears.

3. Drag and drop. Repeat steps 2 and 3 to create as many frames as you want.

4. Adjust the size of each frame by placing your cursor over the separating border so it becomes a double-arrowed icon.

5. Drag and drop.

You can create your pages right now, or place existing pages in the frames you've set up. To do the latter in the easiest way:

1. With your frame-happy page open, open the page you want to place on the frame-happy page and size it so you can see both pages.

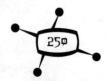

2. With your already-created page active, drag the spider-web icon from the AOLpress toolbar to the frame you want the page to appear in.

2. Drag'n'drop the spiderweb to the frame you wish to link to your page

The new FrameSet page with two frames

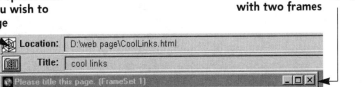

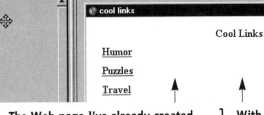

The Web page I've already created   1. **With this page active...**

3. You have successfully created a linked version of your page in one of your frames; any changes to one will automatically be changed in the other.

Saving FrameSet Pages

Next you'll be wanting to save your page, a perfectly reasonable response to all this activity. To save your FrameSet page, you'll want to save each of the frames within the page (click to activate the page within a frame, then press Ctrl+S), then save the FrameSet page itself. To do so:

1. Hover your cursor over a frame border to get the double-arrowed icon, then click. The FrameSet will be bordered in magenta.

2. Now press Ctrl+S.

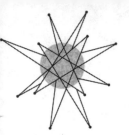

3. In the Save As dialog box, the actual file name (contained within the pathway in the Page Location field—I know, it's confusing) will be highlighted. Just type the name you really want to give the FrameSet page and click OK.

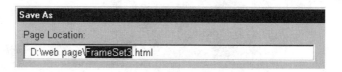

Save As

Page Location:

D:\web page\FrameSet3.html

TIP

If you're cruising merrily along, saving here and there, and suddenly you don't like the last string of things you did to your FrameSet page, you can undo all the changes you made since your last Save in one fell swoop by selecting the FrameSet page (two-arrowed icon, magenta border) and, in the AOLpress toolbar, clicking the Reload button. If you're sure you want to revert to the last saved version of your page, press Reload in the confirmation dialog box.

If when you reopen your new FrameSet page you don't see anything but a blank window, don't panic. You haven't lost all your work; you just haven't opened the page in Frame view. To remedy the situation, try one of the following options:

Choose Format ➤ Frames ➤ Show Frames. This fix is temporary; it lasts as long as you have the current page open.

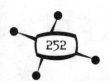

 Choose Tools ➤ Preferences ➤ General. In the General Preferences dialog box, checkmark the Show Frames checkbox. Click OK. This fix will allow you to see frames in all pages that have them.

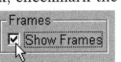

Make sure people enjoying older Web browsers aren't left out in the cold by your frame page; from the AOLpress menu bar, choose Format ➤ Frames ➤ Hide Frames. All you'll see is the FrameSet page without the frames, which is all certain poor souls will see as well. Throw them a bone: some text explaining why they can't see the page they want, a hotlink to a nonframe page, a hotlink to a downloadable frame-supporting Web browser, anything.

WARNING

One of the drawbacks to frames is that viewers can't easily bookmark their contents. A bookmarked frame site will always open to the tops of the original Web pages placed by you in the frame, regardless of where the viewer was when she chose to bookmark the page.

To delete a frame, click inside that page to activate that frame, and then, from the AOLpress menu bar, choose Format ➤ Frames ➤ Delete Frame.

Linking with Targets

Targets are links that point to specific frame pages. Say, for argument's sake, you've created an outline in one frame and informative text that expands on that outline in another frame, as I have

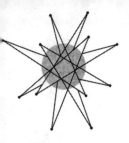

on my Cool Links Web page. You'll want to allow viewers the luxury of checking out the outline, then clicking the hotlink they're interested in following. Because you've framed this whole experience, the hotlink will take them to the place in the second frame that discusses that particular topic. To enable this scenario, you'll need to set targets.

To create a target, first you need to name the frame you're targeting. You may think you already have named it, but you've only titled it and located it using a file name.

To name a frame:

1. Click the frame you wish to name to make it the active frame (if your plans include a stable outline on one side and, on the other, the text the outline links to, you'll want to name the latter frame).

2. From the menu bar, choose Format ➤ Frames ➤ Frame Info.

3. In the Frame Info dialog box, make sure the URL matches the filename of the frame you selected (if it doesn't, you most likely selected something else; just go back and select the frame you want). In the Name field, type **main**.

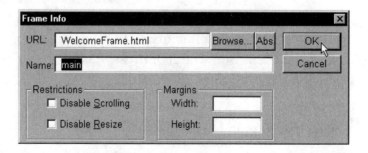

4. You could substitute anything for *main*, as long as it's a name you'll remember.

5. Click OK.

Okay! You're ready to create some links.

1. Choose the text in your stable (e.g., outline) frame that you want to link to another page.

2. From the menu bar, click Element ➤ Link.

3. Browse to the file you want to display in your other frame; when you find it, click OK.

4. Now, in the Target Frame field, click the drop-down arrow.

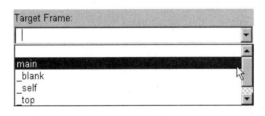

5. Notice that you have *main*, or whatever name you gave your second, linking frame, as your top choice, followed by some stock choices (these are preceded by little underscores; I'll explain them later).

6. Choose main, then click OK.

7. Test it by clicking your linking text; your new page should show up in the frame you specified, as did mine in Figure 8.7.

If you want to link from your frame page to someone else's site, you won't want it to show up in a frame. To specify that the linked-to site should open up its own page, you can use the stock commands in the Target Frame field.

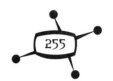

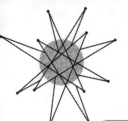

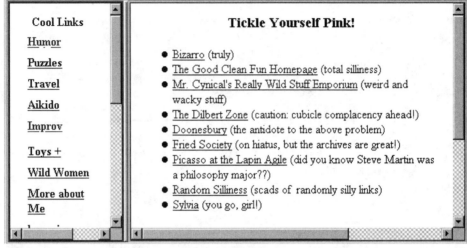

Tickle Yourself Pink!

Cool Links

Humor

Puzzles

Travel

Aikido

Improv

Toys +

Wild Women

More about
Me

- Bizarro (truly)
- The Good Clean Fun Homepage (total silliness)
- Mr. Cynical's Really Wild Stuff Emporium (weird and wacky stuff)
- The Dilbert Zone (caution: cubicle complacency ahead!)
- Doonesbury (the antidote to the above problem)
- Fried Society (on hiatus, but the archives are great!)
- Picasso at the Lapin Agile (did you know Steve Martin was a philosophy major??)
- Random Silliness (scads of randomly silly links)
- Sylvia (you go, girl!)

FIGURE 8.7: A good laugh alleviates most ills.

WARNING

If you don't specify either a new page or another frame for the linked-to page, this page will be displayed in the frame from which you linked. In my example, that would be the thin frame containing the outline text. Because the purpose of this frame is to be a stable entity that visitors can always refer to, you definitely don't want it to be linked away from.

The stock commands you can choose for the Link dialog box's Target Frame field are:

_blank   The new page will open in a separate window. If you specify this for all your pages, links will keep opening more and more new windows.

_self   The linked-to page will show up in the same frame as the link. Not ideal unless your initial frame page consists of a lot of outlines and you want that sort of confusion.

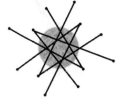

_top   The frames will be removed from your page and the linked-to page will open in this new nonframe window. Use this to link to other people's Web sites. (You and visitors can click the Back arrow to return to your frame page. Your frame page still exists: _top is a way of opening a _blank page but not having two Web pages open.)

_parent   This command refers to the FrameSet page itself; very complicated frame pages might contain a *parent* FrameSet page and an embedded *child* FrameSet page. The _parent specification would open the new Web page in the parent FrameSet page. If you're going to try this, you'll want to brush up on your HTML.

Got that? Speaking of HTML, let's discuss it briefly.

WORKING WITH HTML

One excellent way to gain more flexibility within your Web page is to look at the HTML codes on other peoples' pages. AOLpress makes this really easy; just surf to a Web page you admire and, in AOLpress' toolbar, choose Tools ➤ Show HTML. A second page displaying the Web page's HTML tags will open up on top of your browser-view window. Highlight and copy anything (within reason dictated by taste and copyright law) you want to use.

THE VERY BASICS OF HTML

Web pages start with <html> and end with </html>. Within these tags, information about the page is surrounded by <head> and </head>; the title bar's title with <title> and </title>; and the main part of the page, including text paragraphs, images, and links, with <body> and </body>.

You're getting the picture here; each item on a Web page is begun by a command (e.g., body) and ended by its cease-and-

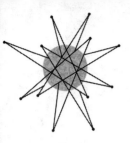

desist command (e.g., /body). The browser knows the command is a command and not just text because commands are enclosed in angle brackets: < > .

Between the <body> and </body> tags, you can go wild:

 Headings: <h1> </h1> start it off; <h2>, <h3>, <h4>, <h5>, and <h6> get smaller and smaller

 Paragraph: <p>*paragraph text*</p>

Image file: <img src="filename.gif">

Link: <a href="filename.html">*link text*</a>

Crazy-making: <blink>*text or image*</blink>

HTML tags can be uppercase, lowercase, or a mixture of both; it doesn't matter to the Web browser.

If you want to explore HTML further, I recommend two books: *HTML: No Experience Required.* (Mack and Platt; Sybex, 1997) and *Mastering HTML* (Deborah Ray and Eric Ray; Sybex, 1997).

THE SECRET TO CHANGING FONTS

Typeface aficionados will be disappointed to see that there's no built-in font flexibility with AOLpress (except for *fixed pitch*, more commonly known as monospaced font—which I wouldn't really call flexible).

Continued

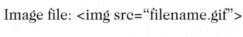
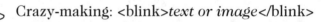

However, you can change fonts by playing with your page's HTML coding. To do so:

1. Open the Web page you wish to alter.

2. From the menu bar, choose Tools ➤ Show HTML.

3. Place your cursor just before the text you wish to display in your chosen typeface.

4. Type the following:

   <font face="*font*">

   where *font* is the name of the typeface you want to display.

5. Place your cursor just after the text to be displayed in this typeface.

6. Type **</font>**.

Just to be safe—and to include viewers using all types of operating systems—you might want to research the font names used by Macs and PCs and include both if a font is called two different things, such as Arial/Helvetica. To cover your bases, you'd type

<font face="Arial,Helvetica">*the Helvetica text enclosed between the two tags*</font>

in Step 4. The viewer's browser would display the text in whichever font was recognized by the visitor's computer.

Remember to use common fonts that people are likely to have on their systems. If you must use wild and wacky fonts, create that part of your page as an image (and don't forget—you can use image mapping to simulate text links).

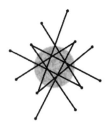

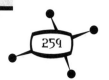

To make sure the changes you make in your HTML window will work, choose File ➤ Parse from the menu bar. AOLpress will check your HTML code for errors and alert you if it finds any. If all you get is a dialog box proclaiming *done*, click OK, then click the HTML page's Close button at the upper right. Your changes will show up on your WYSIWYG Web page.

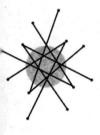

TIP

To clean the slate of your latest HTML madness and start from the pristine state your HTML was in before the current round of coding, just choose File ➤ Reload without SSI from the menu bar.

The MiniWeb: Tracking and Organizing Your Pages

Ready to check out what sort of spiderweb you've created? Mini-Webs are great ways to get a visual feel for all the links going into and out of your site. To create a MiniWeb:

1. Open a page in AOLpress (any page, as long as the expanded menu bar is visible).

2. Choose Tools ➤ Webize Directory.

3. In the Webize Directory dialog box, navigate to the directory you want to create a MiniWeb from.

4. Click the Webize button.

Continued

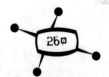

5. You'll be treated to a visual of your pages as they stand so far; with your MiniWeb, you can decide whether your hierarchy makes sense, see what links are broken, move things around via drag'n'drop...

This file has been uploaded to your Web site

This file still rests on your hard drive

Image map

Choose Print Graph to print your MiniWeb

Zoom in, zoom out, and hide selected file types

View as Web, as you see here

View file names alphabetically

View by Web page file name—a bit like an outline

Check links

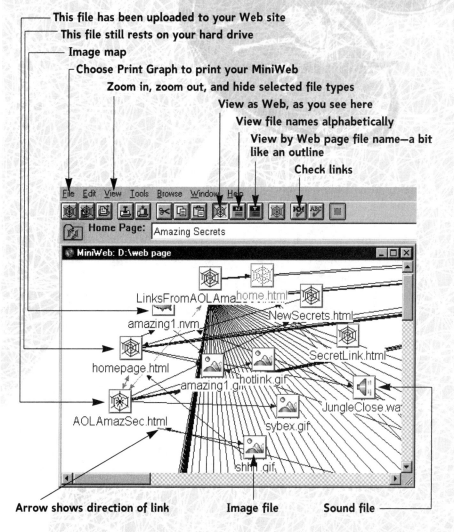

Arrow shows direction of link   **Image file**   **Sound file**

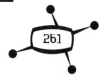

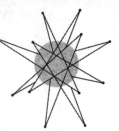

PUBLISHING YOUR PAGE

Now that you've created this complex set of awesome pages, you'll want to put them in your Internet space (My Place).

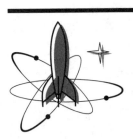

TIP

Whatever you type in the Title field will show up in the title bar your visitors see. Be goofy or be relevant, but just be aware.

Ready? Here we go:

1. Sign onto AOL.

2. Start AOLpress.

3. Rev your engines...oh, sorry. Wrong book. Open the Web page you wish to post and, from the AOLpress menu bar, choose File ➤ Save As.

4. In the Page Location field, type **http://members.aol.com/ YourScreenName/index.html**. Notice that the Drives/ Sites field shows `http://members.aol.com/` as the destination for this particular save.

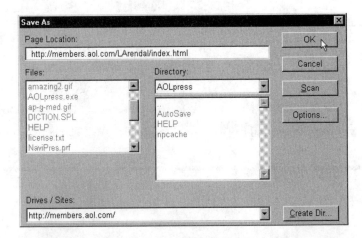

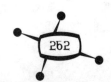

NOTE

You must keep the *index.html* ending for your home page because *index* is the only name AOL will recognize as the starting point for anyone attempting to view your Web page. You may wonder: well, then isn't the full URL I need to give people actually `http://members.aol.com/`*screenname*`/index.html`? You could give them the whole shebang, but you don't have to. `Http://members.aol.com/`*screenname* will automatically go to the index.html page first.

5. Click OK.

6. Be patient; file transfer will take a little time. Watch the Egyptian icons twirl, think about what you'll name your auxiliary pages, read ahead in this book…

7. The page you see in the AOLpress window is now your Web page! Switch to AOL (using Windows' taskbar) for a different browser's take on your page and navigate to your home page. It may take a minute or two, but it should show up at `http://members.aol.com/`*YourScreenName*.

8. Do you like it? Do you see things you want to adjust (forgot a space here, a period there)? Just go back to AOL-press, close your Web page, and open the file from your hard drive.

9. Make any adjustments necessary and follow the above steps to repost your page to the Internet. A dialog box will warn you that the file already exists; because you are intentionally editing and replacing the file, click Save. To see your updated page with AOL, click your Web browser's Reload button.

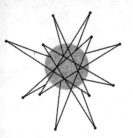

And so on. Repeat the above steps to post all the pages comprising your Web site to your Internet space. Remember to use a unique name for each page you post so you don't accidentally overwrite another page.

NOTE

To get more help with AOLpress, go to keyword **aolpress** and either read through the online documentation or try the AOLpress Help Station, from where you can post to the AOLpress message board or participate in AOLpress chat and classes.

CREATING AND FINDING ART FOR YOUR WEB PAGE

The following sections will help you find fabulous prefab art, get your photos into browsable form, and find and use software to create your own wild (or beautiful—or both) art.

CLIP ART

Clip art is easy, quick, and a great find for those who don't wish to display their artistic talent (or what they perceive as lack thereof). You lose customizability, of course, unless you alter the image with a paint program (in which case it becomes something other than clip art, a sort of a clip art demon child).

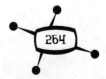

You Say GIF, I Say JPEG...

The two most common image file formats used on the Web are GIF and JPEG.

GIF is the most commonly used format; GIF images contain up to 256 colors, they're flexible, and they're perfect for computer-generated images.

JPEGs are used for photographs and for images that don't have large areas of solid color. They can contain up to 16 million different colors, but they are remarkably small; they achieve their tiny stature by deleting information that the human eye won't notice.

WARNING

There's art all over AOL and the Web, but, as I've said before, be careful about copyright. Basically, anyone who comes up with an idea—whether the idea be expressed in words, images, or something else—can copyright that creative expression just by saying so. If a Web site says it's copyrighted, go somewhere else. If you really, really want to reproduce a copyrighted piece, ask the owner's permission. If the owner says yes, include a line attributing the work to its owner. If the owner says no, respect that and go away.

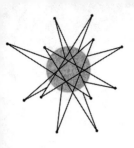

The AOLpress Clip Art Gallery

First take a look at AOLpress' clip art at `http://www.AOLpress` `.com/gallery/`. This site has some pretty cool art arranged in templates that you may copy and use as you wish. It even has some "Created with AOLpress" logos, which come complete with a hotlink to AOLpress itself, that you can include in your site.

To copy AOLpress' clip art to your hard drive:

1. With AOLpress, navigate to the AOLpress Clip Art Gallery at `http://www.AOLpress.com/gallery/`.

2. Check out your options; when you've found art you like, such as the Picasso-esque hands shown here, choose File ➤ Save As.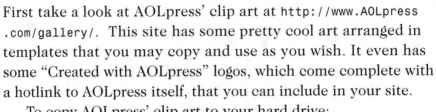

3. In the Save As dialog box (Figure 8.8) that comes up, first choose the drive you want to save the art file on (you can save it online, but it's easiest to edit your pages on your hard drive, so I'd recommend downloading it).

4. Next, navigate to the directory you want to save the image file in.

5. Lastly, check the Page Location field and adjust the image name if necessary. If, for instance, it's called index.html, you may want to rename it picasso.html.

Note

In the Save As dialog box, the image name is the portion of the pathway after the last backslash.

6. Click OK. The image you now see in the AOLpress window looks like it hasn't changed, but it is in actuality the version you've downloaded to your hard drive and is an

editable page like any other AOLpress Web page. Which can mean only one thing: play time! Move the images around, delete the ones you don't want, type your text in between images; the page is your oyster.

3. Change the file name if you like

2. Navigate to the directory you want

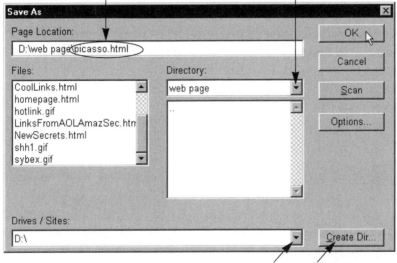

1. Choose your drive   Create a new directory

FIGURE 8.8: Save and play.

Quick Clips

The Quick Clips site has a bunch of colorful graphics, bullets, lines, and some alphabets ready for appropriation. Go to http://www .aol.com/images/public/, pick your image, and click it to get to the HTML code for that icon.

To place this image on your Web page:

1. Copy the HTML coding directly beneath the image you want; it should look something like

    ```
    <imgsrc="http://www.aol.com/images/public/bulletdir/
    bullets/bullet28.gif" height="40" width="40" alt="-">
    ```

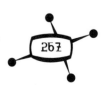

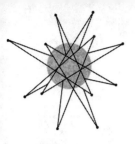

2. In AOLpress, open your Web page you want the clip art to display on.

3. Place your cursor where you want the image to appear.

4. Open the HTML version of the page (Tools ➤ Show HTML).

5. Paste the HTML code into your page.

6. Parse to make sure you haven't interrupted another set of codes.

7. Close the HTML window; your new quick clip will glow brightly on your page.

8. Save it if you like it, move it around in HTML view (or delete it) if you don't.

The Web Art Resource Center

Go to keyword **webart** for this most excellent center for the arts; you can watch short movies about creating special effects (Want your yummy words to look edible? Chocolatize them!), be inspired by art other AOLies have created (some of this is even freely distributable, but do check carefully), as well as get some design know-how under your belt. This site is a must if you enjoy computer-aided graphic art.

To check out the member-created art at this Center, click on one of these

to get to a list of downloadable image files.

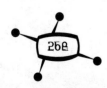

	Upld	Subject	Count	Download
	11/25/97	GIF: Sign My Guestbook Button	1093	1/18/98
	11/25/97	GIF: Guestbook	506	1/18/98
	11/25/97	GIF: Sign & View Guestbook	952	1/18/98
	11/25/97	GIF: Email Button	2780	1/18/98
	11/25/97	GIF: Click Here	1117	1/18/98
	11/25/97	GIF: Blue E-Mail Icon	1568	1/18/98
	11/25/97	GIF: File Folders	590	1/18/98
	11/25/97	GIF: Listen Icon	894	1/18/98
	11/25/97	24BIT: Floppy Disk	507	1/18/98
	11/25/97	GIF: Little Skull	2003	1/18/98
	11/25/97	GIF: Small Music Clef	1545	1/18/98

Double-click on an item in the list you want to read about:

GIF: Blue E-Mail Icon

Subject: GIF: Blue E-Mail Icon
Author: Rellicks
Uploaded By: Rellicks
Date: 11/25/97

File: BEMAIL.GIF (5954 bytes)
Estimated Download Time (28800 baud): < 1 minute
Download Count: 1568

Needs: A GIF Viewer

Keywords: Rellicks, EPaint, Web Art, WWW, Internet, Icon, CB

Type: Copyright

[Download Now] [Download Later] [Ask The Staff] [Related Files]

Be sure to check this line carefully; it could say *Copyright*, it could say *Distribute Freely*

The Desktop & Web Publishing Forum

At keyword **pcdwp** (a mouthful—or is that fingerful?) you'll find plenty of Web publishing resources, including message boards (that helpful community's always just around the corner), a Web publishing classroom, and resources for productive dilly-dallying on your page on a rainy Sunday: Java info, HTML basics, animated GIF help, and so on.

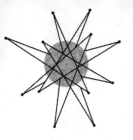

ELSEWHERE

Try using AOL NetFind to search for *images* or for an image category (like *dogs*). You may find some freely distributable clip art.

Alternatively, search for clip art catalogs and, if you find clip art you like, consider investing in a CD. Not only will you have given some starving artist somewhere the means to have an extra cup of coffee with his morning croissant, you'll have a worry-free way to put images that are consistent in their design all over your site.

PHOTOS

Getting your photos scanned is pretty easy these days; your local photo processing place's services may include digitizing the photos created from the negatives you bring in, in which case you'll get back your pictures plus a disk containing your scanned photos.

If you can't find a place locally, take it to the Web; find your favorite photo processor online (Kodak, Fuji, what have you) and tune into their scanning and digitizing options.

Do take some time to look around the Image Scanning Resource Center at keyword **scanning**. The Scanning Services link connects you to the AOL Classifieds, where you can look for a used scanner if that's your bent. The Center also includes message boards (of course), links to scanning hardware and software vendors, and a section of hints and tricks.

CREATING YOUR OWN ART

You can draw and paint in all sorts of programs; Windows comes with Paint, in which you can draw simple bitmap pictures or create tiles for backgrounds. You can also purchase software for simple artwork, like Broderbund's KidPix, for a reasonable price.

Whatever you use, you'll need to save your work as a GIF file.

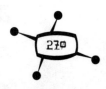

A SCANNER AND PHOTOSHOP SECRET...

In the spirit of "to make sure it's done right; do it yourself", I present to you the really, really basic using-a-scanner-hooked-up-to-a-computer-running-Adobe-Photoshop instructions:

1. Lift the cover of the scanner. Place your photo with a corner at the 0,0 axis of the scanner's rulers.

2. Close the cover (duh).

3. Open Photoshop on the computer connected to the scanner.

4. From the Photoshop toolbar, choose File ➤ Import ➤ Scan (this last choice will show up as different things—like ART-SCAN—depending on your scanning software).

5. In the Scan window, make sure the clickable border encloses your photo without cutting any of it off (you may want to preview the scan). In the Desired Resolution field, be kind to your viewers and their never-fast-enough modems; choose a resolution around 72. It's not the best, but your image will download at a reasonable rate.

6. Click the Scan button. Wait. Wait some more.

7. Photoshop will scan in the photo as well as some whitespace around it; choose the Marquee tool and surround the photo, or the area within the photo you wish to preserve, and click Image ➤ Crop.

8. Choose File ➤ Save. Make sure the Format field shows JPEG, and save your fresh new image to a disk (or to the hard drive or network, depending on where you're doing the scanning). In the resultant JPEG Options box, choose a low quality of 1 or 2 to conserve K's.

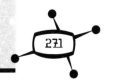

THE SECRET TO SAVING
IMAGES AS GIFS USING AOL

Amazing but true: you don't need to invest in fancy imaging software to convert your bitmap files to GIFs (or JPEGs) for use on the Web! To create an image, then make it Web-worthy:

1. Draw your image in Paint (for instance) and click Save. The picture will be saved as a bitmap (the only image format available to you in Paint).

2. Close Paint.

3. Open AOL (no need to log on).

4. From the menu bar, choose File ➤ Open.

5. In the Open a File dialog box, navigate to your Paint file (its extension will be BMP), select it, and click Open.

6. AOL's picture editor will open with your picture proudly displayed.

7. From AOL's menu bar, now choose File ➤ Save As.

8. Click the arrow next to the Save as Type field at the bottom of the dialog box; notice you have three real choices: BMP, GIF, and JPG. Choose GIF (unless you want JPG).

9. Click Save. Your picture is now ready to survive the stormy Internet seas!

Continued

Notice you have a row of editing tools available to you (if you don't see these, click the Show/Hide Tools arrow in the picture editor's upper-left corner).

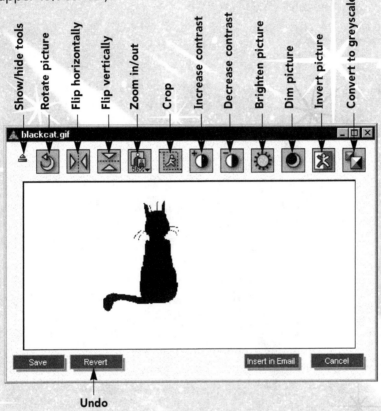

Undo

NOTE

The Web Art Resource Center points to some good shareware for constructing animated GIFs, which are basically a sequence of separate GIF files strung together and opened, one after the other in a continuous loop, on your Web page.

TIPS TO HELP YOU FINISH UP

Following are some odds and ends that will be helpful in refining and expanding your Web site:

NOTE

If you want to edit one of your Web pages online or publish an edited or new page to your Web site, you'll need to be logged on to AOL with the screen name the Web site was originally uploaded under.

 Although you only have 2MB of Internet space per screen name, you really have a total of 10MB of space; you can create a mega-Web site by linking all your screen names' sites together.

 Through the members.aol.com Web Administrator, you can keep track of how many times your Web site gets visited by adding a Site Activity Counter. Navigate to `http://members.aol.com/wwwadmin/index .htm`; from here you can add a counter, create a guestbook, keep track of scheduled server maintenance times, and more.

 If you keep all your Web site pages on your hard drive, you'll be able to easily modify a page at your discretion, then upload it to your Web site again. If you choose to keep everything online, you'll need to download your page to modify it, which could take some time, depending on how much traffic is coursing through AOL at that moment.

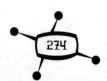

Tips to Help You Finish Up

 If you—accidentally or purposefully—try to modify a Web site other than your own, you will be denied access. To modify a site, you must be signed on as the screen name that uploaded the Web site in the first place.

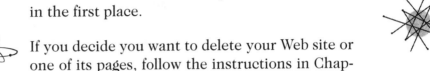 If you decide you want to delete your Web site or one of its pages, follow the instructions in Chapter 1 for deleting files from your FTP site.

MAKING YOUR SITE KNOWN

Now that you've created and posted your masterfully designed Web site, you'll want people to see it. Besides sending e-mail to your family and friends, you can add keywords to your site and submit your URL to your favorite search engines for inclusion in their search archives.

To add keywords to your site:

1. Open your home page in HTML view.

2. Place your cursor within the <head> element after the </title> tag.

3. Press return to start a new line, and type the following:

```
<meta name="keywords" content="place up to 1,000 charac-
ters of synonyms here that people might search for sep-
arated, by, commas, if, you, get, my, drift">
<meta name="description" content="Description of your
site here.">
```

4. Notice that there is no end period after the list of keywords (and that keywords are all separated by commas). Each meta tag's contents should be about 1,000 characters or fewer; some search engines will cut off everything after the first 1,024 letters and spaces.

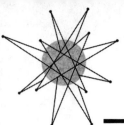

WARNING

While you do want to use as many synonyms as possible in your keyword tag, don't repeat words. Some search engines will refuse to list a repeating-keyworded site if the search-engine programmers felt that keyword repetition is a cheap way to gain more prominence in a search result listing—which it is.

To submit your URL to search engines:

1. Go to the Submit It! Web site at `http://www.submit-it.com`.

2. Click the Submit It! Free list item (if you want to pay for some serious distribution, click instead the Submit It! Online list item).

3. Fill out the form at the bottom of the page. If you don't want your site to appear on any of the search engines listed just above the form, click to undo that box's checkmark. (Of course, not all the big sites are listed; the service is free, after all.)

4. Click the OK, Move On to the Submitting Area button.

5. After you verify that the info you typed in is correct, scroll down and click the Submit It! button next to each of the search engines you picked. Some engines will allow you to state the category your site falls into.

A couple of other Web sites that promote Web site visibility are:

 The Rail at `http://www.therail.com/cgi-bin/station`: here you can connect your site with other Web sites; Web surfers can and do take virtual tours along The Rail.

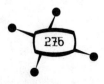

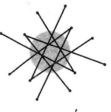

 The Art of Business Web Site Promotion at `http://www.deadlock.com/promote/`: here you can read up on how businesses get their names out there.

OTHER WEB PUBLISHING TOOLS

Though AOLpress is a pretty complete package, you might want to search for and check out other HTML editors such as:

HotMetal

Hot Dog

HomeSite

WebThing

WebPen

HTML Assistant

If you do decide to use a non-AOL Web publishing tool to create your Web site, you can still upload it to AOL. The instructions for doing so read very similarly to the instructions for uploading a file to your FTP space.

To upload to your Internet space a Web page that was created by a program other than Personal Publisher or AOLpress:

1. Sign onto AOL and go to keyword **my place**.

2. Click the Go to My Place button.

3. Click Upload. The Remote Filename dialog box will pop up.

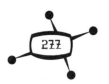

4. Type in the file name of the Web page you wish to upload. For instance, if one of your Web pages is called Welcome.html, you'll want to type **Welcome.html** into this field. (If you rename the file, the hotlinks to it won't work.)

5. Click the ASCII radio button, then click Continue.

6. In the Upload File dialog box, click Select File.

7. In the File Selection dialog box, double-click your Web page file and click OK.

8. Check the pathway that appears in the Upload File dialog box; if it looks right to you, click Send.

And there you have it. One more piece of electronic data added to the ephemeral information superhighway.

Netscape

Though your built-in AOL browser is Internet Explorer, you can use Netscape for your Web prowls; just go to keyword **netscape** and follow the downloading instructions provided there. Keep in mind that Netscape will show up as a separate program on your desktop, but you'll need to be signed on to AOL to use it.

Now that you have a good grounding in all the fun and practical things you can do with AOL, let's take the show on the road!

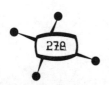

Chapter 9

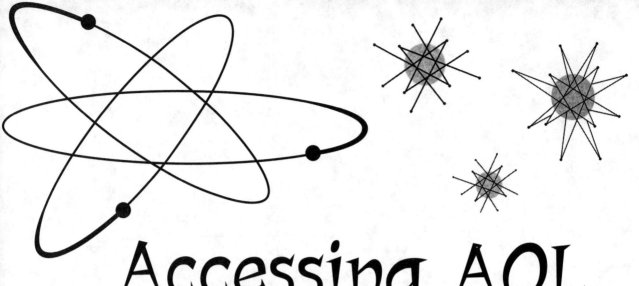

Accessing AOL at Home and on the Road

So you're ready to explore some access options. I'm going to assume that you've already installed AOL and walked through the whole Setup Wizard process that lets you establish the primary and secondary phone numbers your modem connects to AOL with.

NOTE

If you are having problems with the initial connection process, see the Appendix for Help information.

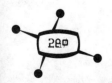

In this chapter you'll explore the exotic savannahs of domestic and international travel as well as tiptoe lightly through the wild internal jungle of modems and other connection devices. In addition, you'll get a peek at some interesting connection possibilities through AOL's BYOA (Bring Your Own Access) option.

ACCESS, THE OLD-FASHIONED WAY

If you've installed AOL successfully, you've already established your connection via 28.8- or 33.6-baud modem and phone line (quaint, but it works). To edit your phone number (maybe you're experiencing too many busy signals with your current access phone number), location (moving?), or modem choice (say you've finally upgraded from that 9600-baud snail to a 33.6 screamer), take the actions outlined in the following sections.

ADDING AN ACCESS PHONE NUMBER

The access numbers you set up originally might not work as well as you'd like. Too many busy signals, too much line noise, whatever! To add to the phone numbers your modem dials to access AOL from home:

1. Sign off from AOL and click the Setup button at the bottom of your Sign On screen. (You can also accomplish something of the same thing by clicking Find ➤ AOL Access Numbers, but I'm partial to signing off.)

   SETUP

2. You'll be rewarded by the Connection Setup dialog box, shown in Figure 9.1.

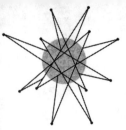

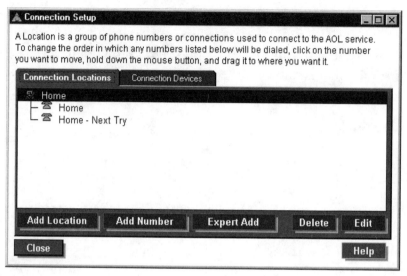

FIGURE 9.1:   Home is where the AOL is.

NOTE

If instead you get the Connection Wizard, just click Expert Setup to get to the Connection Setup dialog box.

3. From here you can rule your modem! Not as much fun as ruling the world, but that can't be helped. Select a new number by clicking the Add Number button.

4. At the first dialog box, enter your area code as requested and click

Country: [United States   ▼] (click to view)

Area Code: [510] (Example: 703)

Next. These boxes should look familiar to you; they're

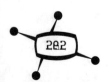

how you established access to AOL the very first time you set up your connection.

5. Next, search through the scrollable list on the left for an access number that is both local and matches (or exceeds) your modem speed.

N0TE

There's no point in purchasing a 33.6-baud modem only to forbid it to run at speeds higher than 28.8K. You can, however, permit it to run at speeds it can only dream about; for instance, by choosing an access number that can connect at 57,600K.

6. When you've found a match, select the number and click the Add button. Check the number in the ensuing dialog box; if it's satisfactory, click OK. Your new choice will be added to the list of access numbers on the right.

AOL access phone numbers:

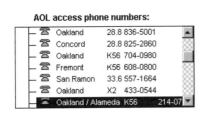

☎ Oakland	28.8	836-5001
☎ Concord	28.8	825-2860
☎ Oakland	K56	704-0980
☎ Fremont	K56	608-0800
☎ San Ramon	33.6	557-1664
☎ Oakland	X2	433-0544
☎ Oakland / Alameda	K56	214-07

ADD

Add numbers to this Location:

Home

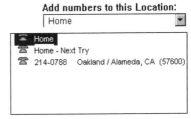

Home
☎ Home - Next Try
☎ 214-0788   Oakland / Alameda, CA (57600)

7. Add away. When you're done, click Done.

As many phone numbers as you add is your assurance that somehow, some way, your modem will connect you to AOL. All the numbers can't be busy at once! Practically speaking, though, you won't often have to resort to a third number to get onto AOL.

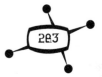

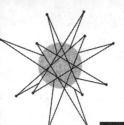

NOTE

If the location you're adding numbers to is in an office building where you need to dial 9 to access an outside line, you'll need to make sure 9- appears at the beginning of the access phone number. See Figure 9.2 for details.

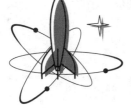

TIP

While it's possible to connect to AOL over a cellular or satellite phone connection, AOL doesn't actually support these connections. If you're skilled at reading between the lines, you'll understand immediately that what this means is, you can do it, but you're on your own if you run into problems. The following Web sites may help: http://www.freeyellow.com/members/myque1/page1.html and http://www.sagem-sat.co.uk/products/ia.htm.

To delete an access number, get into your Connection Setup window (following Steps 1 and 2), highlight the offending number, and click Delete. If you're sure you want to take this drastic measure, click Yes in the confirmation dialog box.

To edit an access number (say you've just signed up for call waiting and you want to make sure your modem's connection doesn't get interrupted), select the number in the Connection Setup window and click Edit to get the dialog box shown in Figure 9.2. If you have multiple numbers associated with a location, you must edit each one separately.

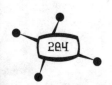

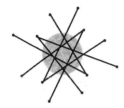

Try this number up to 9 times
before trying another number

Have a different connection use this number
Add this number to another local location

Edit Number (Connection)

Name:
Home - Next Try

Will be added to this location:
Home

Connect using: Modem: Gateway Telepath x2 on COM2

Try to connect 1 time(s) with this number (connection).

Number, exactly as it will be dialed:
628-0331

Edit number here: 628-0331

☐ Dial 9, to reach an outside line. Speed: 38400 bps

☐ Dial *70, to disable call waiting. Network: AOLnet

☑ This phone line has touch-tone service.

OK   Cancel   Help

You'll want to disable call waiting
while you're online so you don't
lose the connection

Make sure the access phone
number you're editing is on
the network you select here:
AOLnet, SprintNet, or (for
most international numbers)
AOLGLOBALnet

Check here if you're in an office
with an internal phone system

Add an area code if necessary—or type
in another access number, if you know it

Choose your modem speed

FIGURE 9.2: It slices, it dices, it edits your access number.

SECRET

While you're waiting for AOL to put your town on the map,
call your long-distance provider and ask whether it offers
any special deals that will allow you to pay a small fee (such
as $10-25) for a certain number of calls per month (100-300
or thereabouts). With a service such as this one, you can stay
online as long as you like; you just need to be careful not to
exceed the allotted number of sign-ons per month.

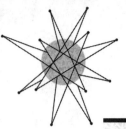

AOL Is Just a Local Phone Call Away

You can access AOL via a local call from a lot of places in the United States. However, the US is pretty big, so there will inevitably be some places for which the nearest access number is actually a toll call.

You'll find a complete list of AOL's local access numbers both from the Connection Setup dialog box and at keyword **access**.

If you can't find a local access number in your area, you can access AOL via AOLnet from either of these numbers:

 1-800-716-0023

1-888-245-0113

However, this solution is only a stop-gap measure, excellent for the avid Automatic AOL user but very expensive for a hardcore onliner (AOL imposes a surcharge—at this writing, of 10 cents per connected minute—on accounts using these numbers).

AOL adds new local numbers constantly, so do check the AOLnet Future Cities listing at keyword **access** from time to time to keep current. In addition, don't hesitate to ask for an AOL number local to you; just double-click the Request Access Numbers icon (also found at keyword **access**).

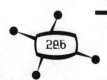

ADDING A NEW LOCATION

You'll want to edit your location when you move or when you're traveling and want to keep tabs on the world through your AOL account. It's much easier to add new locations as you need them than to keep changing the numbers associated with your Home location: you can more easily delete extraneous locations/numbers, and you won't have to fish around for your real home access numbers when you return. To add a location (and its attendant phone numbers):

1. Again, sign off from AOL and click the Setup button at the bottom of your Sign On screen.

2. At the Connection Setup dialog box, click the Add Location button.

3. In the Name field, type in a more descriptive moniker than *Location 2*. *Paris*, maybe, or *Aunt Julia's house*; anything that will help you remember what the set of numbers you'll add for this location refer to.

4. Click Next; you'll be at the same window you saw in Step 4 under *Editing Your Access Phone Number*. Now enter Aunt Julia's area code.

5. From the new list of access numbers, choose as many as you like that are local calls and match or exceed your modem speed, clicking Add after you highlight each one.

AOL access phone numbers:

Add numbers to this Location:

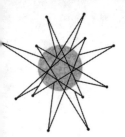

You might have to make a quick call to Aunt Julia or to her local phone company to figure out which of the surrounding towns are actually a local phone call away.

NOTE

Notice that the location, as reported in the Add Numbers to This Location drop-down list box, is now Aunt Julia's house rather than Home. You could, if you wanted, choose Home from here and add numbers to that location as well.

6. Click Done when you're ready.

Now, in the Select Location field of your Sign On window, you have a choice: Home, or the location you just added. Click the drop-down arrow to reveal the list of choices and choose a location from this list to have your modem sign on to AOL with the numbers assigned to that location. You can add as many locations as you're planning on traveling to either before you leave home or on the road.

To delete a location, get back into your Connection Setup window (following Steps 1 and 2), highlight the offending location, and click Delete and confirm.

To edit an existing location, double-click the location name (e.g., Home) in your Connection Setup window. The Edit Location window will appear.

AOL Setup - Home

Edit Location

Name: Home

Try to connect 5 time(s) using each number (connection).

Numbers (Connections) for this Location:

- Home
- Home - Next Try
- 214-0788   Oakland / Alameda, CA (57600)

Add Number   Expert Add   Delete   Edit

OK   Cancel

Here you can dictate the number of tries your modem should make with all the numbers you have attached to this location before giving up the ghost. You can edit or delete highlighted numbers from here (Edit or Delete), add numbers using the walkthrough (Add Numbers), drag'n'drop numbers around if you wish to order them differently, or show off to your friends and family by clicking Expert Add to get to the window shown in Figure 9.3.

The only difference between the Add Number window and the Edit Number window (shown in Figure 9.2) is that here you are confronted by a blank slate as far as the actual access numbers are concerned. Only if you know the appropriate numbers to use should you play with this window.

UPGRADING YOUR MODEM

When you upgrade your modem, you'll want to add, delete, or change the modem you're using. To add a modem:

1. Once again, sign off from AOL and click the Setup button at the bottom of your Sign On screen.

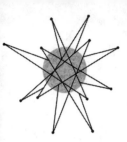

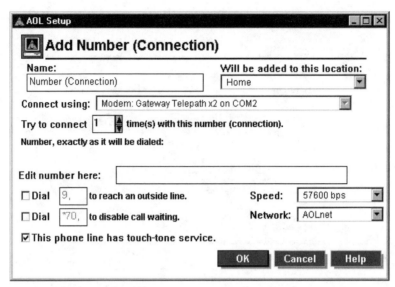

FIGURE 9.3:   Slices, dices, extrudes fresh pasta, and allows you to enter access phone numbers you know.

2.   At the Connection Setup dialog box, click the Connection Devices tab.

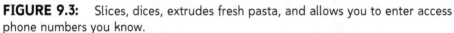

3.   You'll see your modem or other type of connection listed. From here you can click the Auto Detect button to be walked through

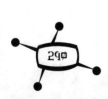

the modem-detection and connection process, which is what I recommend you do.

NOTE

If you're using a high-speed (57.6K) modem, see *High-Speed Modems*, later in this chapter, and/or go to keyword **high speed**.

To delete a modem, highlight it, click Delete, and confirm.

THE SECRET TO ENDING MODEM SCREECHING BY PEACEFUL MEANS

Especially if you're running Automatic AOL sessions in the dead of night when no one's using the computer—or if you time out a lot and have to sign on again fairly often—you'll soon be ready to take a sharp garden implement to your modem if it screeches at you just one more time. Well, you can put that thing right back in the tool shed where you found it, because your troubles are over.

1. Click the Connection Devices tab.

2. Double-click the modem you're using to connect (it'll be marked with a red checkmark).

Connection Locations	Connection Devices
☑ Modem: Gateway Telepath x2 on COM2	

Continued

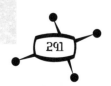

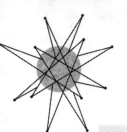

3. You'll get the Expert Edit Modem box. Look, over there in the lower-right corner! It's Speaker Volume! Set to AOL's default of *Normal*! Click the drop-down arrow and change it!

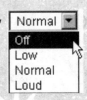

4. Click OK. Blissful silence ensues.

The Expert Upgrade

If you want to dispense with the fuss of auto detect and manual delete in order to connect your upgraded modem to your AOL account, highlight the modem you've gotten rid of and click Edit. The Expert Edit Modem window will appear (don't think too hard about that title), as shown in Figure 9.4.

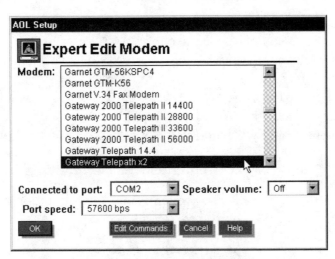

FIGURE 9.4: Is the modem doing the expert editing, or is the Edit Modem an expert?

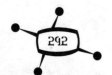

Choose your new modem and click OK. If your modem is not listed, try choosing:

 Hayes Basic

Hayes EC

 Hayes Extended

Hayes Auto-Reliable

If none of these generic modem settings work with your computer—and *if* you want to get super-techy—you can try the following:

1. In your modem's manual, find the command strings for Hardware Flow Control, Data Compression, and Error Correction. Standard commands look like:

   > Hardware Flow Control: &K3 or \Q3
   > Data Compression On: %C1
   > Error Correction On: &Q5
   > Repond to dial tone and busy signal: X4

2. At the AOL Sign-On window, click Setup ➤ Connection Devices tab, double-click on your modem, then click the Edit Commands button.

3. In the Setup Modem String field, highlight the string of characters there and type in the string you've pieced together from your manual, beginning with AT&F and adding an ^M to the end. It might look something like:

   > AT&F&K3%C1&Q5^M

   All the letters should be capitalized, and be careful that any zeros are entered as such, not as the letter *O*.

4. Click OK twice, then Close to get back to the Sign On window. Sign on.

NOTE

Do you care what the modem string categories mean to your modem? AT&F tells your modem to begin paying attention to what's being transmitted. Hardware flow control ensures that your modem's buffer doesn't overflow or disconnect, data compression puts your data in a neat little package for quicker transmittal, error correction works to ensure that your high-speed transmission is error-free, and the ^M thingy is a carriage return that signals to the modem that the command string has ended.

If none of the above approaches work, call Tech Support at 1-800-827-3338 within North America, 1-703-264-1184 if you are not in the US or Canada.

A Word about Modems...

You've certainly noticed that, regardless of your modem's advertised speed, you usually connect to AOL at a lower rate—and that rate varies. The actual connect rate you get depends on how busy the access number is at the time and the quality of your phone line (in addition to the line-noise issue, some phone lines won't support connect rates higher than 28.8K), and it actually varies during your online session depending on the connection and your equipment.

If the files you download from AOL consistently take much longer than indicated in the file's description, you will want to make sure that AOL thinks you're using the modem that you are indeed using. If your connection device is set to a different modem than the one you really are using, AOL—through no fault of its own—will be sending the wrong commands to your modem. See *Upgrading Your Modem*, earlier in this chapter, for the steps to remedy this situation.

High-Speed Modems

If you're an early adopter, you may already have the modem of the future: one of those newfangled 57,600-baud babies. AOL is still testing its 57.6K lines, so though you have the technology to go, go, go, you may still be waiting with the rest of us for the time being.

And, even if AOL is running perfectly smoothly and your phone line is completely interference-free, you will only get a max speed of 53K because that is the highest the FCC will currently allow. The other point to keep in mind is that the high-speed connection rate you get from AOL only applies to transmissions you receive *from* AOL: anything you upload to AOL will be transmitted at 28.8K or slower.

If you're starting to think about upgrading to one of the high-speed modems, you should know that there are two types: x2 and K56flex. AOL supports both these types, and you'll have to make sure you choose the correct type when you go to connect your modem; an x2 modem won't work at high speeds on a K56flex line.

For more information about AOL's high-speed–modem field trials, go to keywords **x2** and/or **k56flex**.

SECRET

Something else you should watch out for is an ISP "local" number that, instead of connecting directly to the ISP, forwards your call to a node, which calls another node, which then calls the ISP. ISPs thus extend their areas, affording a larger number of people local connections. However, call forwarding can slow transmission speeds to as low as 14.4K in order to avoid degrading modem signals. When you choose an ISP, make sure it's really a local ISP.

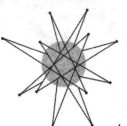

ACCESS VIA AN ISP AND THE BYOA OPTION

Acronym city, huh?! An ISP is an Internet service provider; AOL's BYOA option is its Bring Your Own Access service. Why, you're asking, would any sane person want to pay for two providers when you can just sign up with AOL? There are some advantages. AOL's BYOA option is cheaper than its regular unlimited-access service, but allows you unlimited access to AOL. If your ISP's rates are low, you may save money. However, even if it turns out to be as expensive or slightly more than straight unlimited-access charges, it may be worth it to you because your ISP will use different access numbers than the regular AOL populace. This means you stand an excellent chance of never getting a busy signal while signing on to AOL and you won't have to deal with the 46-minute (and 92-minute, and so on) time-out dialog box.

In addition, if you are connecting from work or school, your connection device will probably be not a modem but a local-area network, which uses TCP/IP, a protocol that allows connections over dedicated non-phone lines at speeds much faster than modems can achieve.

You can research your BYOA options at keyword **byoa**. Some additional tips:

You can access AOL through a SprintNet number, a boon if you are a Sprint customer or are interested in switching to Sprint's phone service. Call Sprint at 1-800-747-9428 or navigate to `http://www.sprint.com/fornet`.

To find a local ISP, navigate to `http://www.thelist.com`. Be sure to look for a provider that offers unlimited access for a monthly fee.

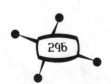

WARNING

After signing up for AOL's BYOA plan, remember to use your ISP to connect to AOL at all times. If you forget and connect to AOL using a regular AOLnet access number, you'll be charged an extra $2.50 per hour (of course, this figure is subject to change).

After you've signed up with an ISP and AOL's BYOA option, follow these steps to set up your ISP-to-AOL connection:

1. At the AOL Sign On window, click Setup, then click the Connection Devices tab.

2. Click Expert Add and, in the Select Type of Communication Device window, click the drop-down list arrow, select TCP/IP, and click Next.

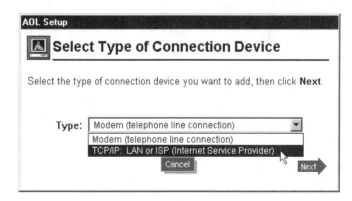

3. At the Expert Add TCP/IP window, uncheck the Sign Onto America Online Now checkbox, and click Next.

4. Back at the Connection Setup window, click the Connection Locations tab. You'll notice TCP/IP has been added to your list of locations.

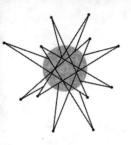
5. Click Close.

6. Connect to your ISP.

7. Leaving your ISP connection active, switch to AOL.

8. Make sure TCP/IP is showing in the Sign On window's Select Location field, and sign on.

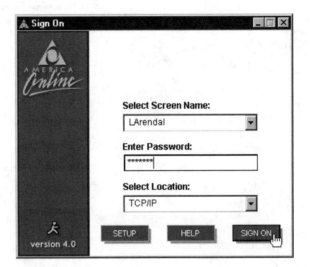

If you need to adjust your proxy configuration (say you're at work and your Tech Guru has set up a security firewall between your network and the Internet), you'll need to edit your TCP/IP connection thusly:

1. From the Sign On window, click Setup, then double-click on TCP/IP from the Connection Locations tab.

2. At the Edit Location window, make sure TCP/IP is selected and click Edit.

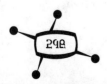

3. At the bottom of the Edit Number (Connection) window, check the Manual Proxy Configuration radio button; the View button will become active.

○ Automatic Connection Script: **Direct TCP/IP Connection**

● **Manual Proxy Configuration:** **View ...**

4. Click View. In the resulting Connection dialog box, click the Connect Using Proxy checkbox, as in Figure 9.5.

FIGURE 9.5: Configure the middle person in your computer's conversation with AOL.

5. Type the name your ISP has provided you in the Proxy Server Host field, make sure the rest of the information matches your ISP's requirements, and click OK three times to close out of the TCP/IP editing windows. Click Close, and you're back at the AOL Sign On window.

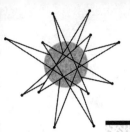

TV + AOL?

If you're moving everything away from your desk and onto your couch, you'll want to look into hooking up your TV cable modem to AOL. Cable modems provide vastly accelerated download times (usually 10MB, with possible speeds of up to 30MB), but many cable lines are not yet configured for two-way service. Therefore, you may still need to use your phone line for regular-speed uploads. Still, one way is better than nothing (can you say *online movie*?)!

To connect to AOL via a cable modem, you'll need to set AOL's Location field to TCP/IP. Just follow the instructions for setting up an ISP connection, then connect to your cable modem service provider and, leaving that connection active, sign onto AOL using TCP/IP.

For more information, go to keyword **cable**.

NOTE

Using an ISDN line to connect to AOL is an option, too, but ISDN lines are expensive and the connection slow relative to cable: about 4 times the price per month and only 128K compared to 10MB per second. Unless you're going to install one for another purpose, like a home business, I don't recommend going to the expense and trouble to do so just for AOL. However, if you already have ISDN access, you can use it to connect to AOL by first connecting to an ISP that supports ISDN, then using the BYOA option and the TCP/IP setting to connect to AOL, as described earlier in this section.

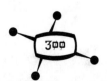

TIP

You can access your AOL mail through another service provider; whether you're at work or at school (but not on AOL), point your Web browser to `http://www.aol.com` and click on NetMail.

TRAVELING WITHIN THE US

I've already run through adding a new location and its new access numbers in *Adding a New Location*, earlier in this chapter. And, if you're not traveling with your own laptop, but your destination's amenities include a computer with an AOL account, you can access your online information (such as incoming mail—as opposed to old mail stored on your hard drive) by signing on as a guest. Guest sign-on is covered in Chapter 1, *Excelling in E-Mail*.

You can, as I've said, determine the access numbers you'll need to use either before you embark or during your travels (see *Adding a New Location*). The advantage to the former is, if you know the number, you can call the phone company ahead of time to inquire whether that number is a local or toll call from the hotel or dwelling where you'll be staying. Thus you will eliminate any nasty surprises down the road.

Another thing to keep in mind when traveling is that you want to make sure to plug your modem line into the correct phone jack. If you're staying at a residence, the phone lines will more than likely be analog, which is the kind you want. Most large hotels offer data or fax lines, which, being analog, will also work.

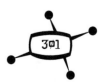

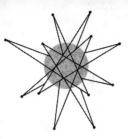

If you don't see a clearly labeled line, make sure that the phone lines are analog. Some hotels may only offer digital phone lines (these support multi-optioned phones), and you can't use a digital phone line with your modem. If a digital line is the only thing available to you, you can buy an adapter at your local Compu-Everything-but-the-Kitchen-Sink store.

TRAVELING OUTSIDE THE US

If you're going to visit your old college roommate in Norway, but you've got some work you need to get done while you're there (or you just want to stay connected to your family while you're away), you can set up a new connection location for Norway quite easily from your Connection Setup window. To set up an international location:

1. Sign off from AOL and click the Setup button at the bottom of your Sign On screen.

2. At the Connection Setup dialog box (shown way back in Figure 9.1), click Add Location, then type in a name for this location (your friend's name, for example).

3. Make sure the Add Numbers from a List of Access Phone Numbers radio button is selected, then click Next.

4. In the Search for Access Numbers dialog box that next appears, select the country you're adding from the Country drop-down list.

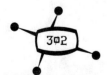

5. Depending on what country you're adding, you may get a few or many numbers to choose from. Choose a city close to your friend that offers a connection speed equal to or greater than your modem's speed, and add that number to your new location.

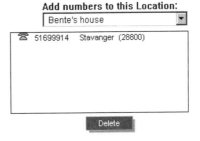

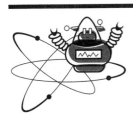

WARNING

If you highlight a number and click the More Info button, you'll see that most international numbers use the AOL-GLOBALnet network. AOLGLOBALnet use brings with it a surcharge to your account. Moreover, if you're planning on using Expert Add to add any international numbers to a location, you'll want to make sure you know which are AOLGLOBALnet and which AOLnet so you can indicate the proper network on the Expert Edit Modem screen.

6. When you've picked the numbers you wish to use, click the Done arrow.

You can also search for an appropriate access number by checking out keyword **aolglobalnet** or keyword **aolnet**.

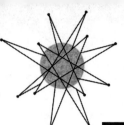

TIP

You'll be prompted to add at least two numbers, even if you're going to a relatively remote location like Norway, which only has three access numbers in the whole country. After you've added it here, you can go back to the Connection Setup window and just delete the number you don't want. (Alternatively, you could add the same number twice.)

If you have difficulty connecting to AOL while you're traveling abroad (say you can't find an access number or your modem won't recognize the dial tone), call the AOL International Access Support Team at (1)703-264-1184—or fax them at (1)801-622-7901. At this writing, staff is available to help you at any time.

Which brings me to my next topic; Help! For information on fixing anything about your AOL experience, turn the page.

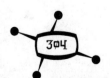

Appendix A

Help!

Though at times you may feel adrift in a sea of voices and endless AOL areas, you are never far from guidance and advice should you need it. There are quite a few ways to get help for any problem you might encounter, from computer difficulties to interpersonal problems to AOL service stumpers. Following is a quick and dirty list of the various ways to get help; I'll discuss each of them thoroughly in the forthcoming pages.

WHERE TO GO TO GET IT

If you're having trouble with some aspect of the AOL service, try the remedies below in order of appearance. The list is organized in descending order of ease of use and need. In other words, it's very easy to access Offline Help, and it'll help you with general questions. On the other hand, because it can be difficult to get through to a live human being and being on hold is something you'll want to subject yourself to only out of sheer desperation, calling AOL's customer service line is way down at the bottom.

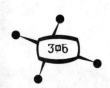

In order, then:

Offline Help   Before you sign on, you'll find info about signing on, how to use AOL's features, security, and trouble-shooting modem and access problems. From the menu bar, select Help ➤ Offline Help and choose the topic(s) you want information on.

Online Help   Once you're online, you find pertinent help information from the Help menu. You'll have access to:

 Member Services Online Help topics: Before you wait in a virtual or auditory line for technical assistance, try reading up on the help topics posted in the Member Services area.

 phone numbers for accessing AOL through various means (another service provider, 800 number, from abroad, etc.)

your billing info

Parental Controls

hints on using keywords

the skinny on what's new in AOL 4

New Member Help   If you're an AOL newbie, don't despair. Even though AOL is super easy to figure out, everyone can use a push in the right direction. To get the new-member lowdown, type keyword **quickstart** into the Keyword/URL box and press Go.

Using Find   On the far right of the toolbar, under the People icon, you'll see the Find button. Using the Find

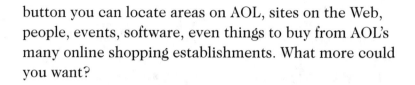

button you can locate areas on AOL, sites on the Web, people, events, software, even things to buy from AOL's many online shopping establishments. What more could you want?

Message Boards   There is an unthreatening place on AOL where no question is a stupid question: the message boards. Type in keyword **mhm** and click Go to be connected to the help underground. Click on Message Boards, and you'll be greeted by a list of topics for which there are many posted questions. The people who post questions to these message boards are AOL members. The people who answer these questions are also AOL members. Hence the keyword: MHM stands for Members Helping Members.

Area-Specific Help   If you need assistance with your software or hardware, want to know more about an AOL area, or want to chat with other divorcees with kids, you can find that sort of help too. Just go to the area that fits the topic and find its FAQ (frequently asked questions), chat room, or advice line.

Tech Help via e-mail   If reading canned info and talking to other AOLies doesn't solve your dilemma, online technical help is your next step. First navigate through Help ➤ Member Services Online Help ➤ Help Topic of your choice. Click on the Ask the Staff button on the lower left and choose to contact the tech staff via e-mail, option number two on the Live Technical Support menu.

Member Help Interactive   If your question is of a general nature, try the member-volunteer–hosted auditorium. Navigate to Help ➤ Member Services Online Help ➤ Help Topic of your choice. Click on the Ask the Staff button on

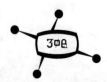

the lower left and choose option number three, the Tech Live Auditorium (someone will be online early in the day until quite late in the evening). Don't overlook it; it's way better than waiting on the phone.

TOS Help   As I've covered in Chapters 2 and 3, if you have trouble with anyone who is violating AOL's Terms of Service agreement, go to keyword **TOS** and report them.

Phone Numbers   But if you *gotta* wait on the phone, you'll want to find the right number so you don't have to wait in line twice. I list these phone numbers at the very end of this appendix. If you don't find the one you need, go to Help ➤ Member Services Online Help ➤ Help Topic of your choice ➤ Ask the Staff for a list of AOL staff telephone numbers. If you can't get online, just call Customer Support at 1-800-827-3338 (someone will be there from early in the day to quite late in the evening).

HELP ADVICE AND SECRETS

As promised, what follows is more in-depth discussion of the different help options available to you, plus, of course, some secrets. I've listed each option in the same order as above.

GENERAL HELP FROM AOL FILES

Don't underestimate the knowledge you can gain from reading. I confess I'm as guilty as anyone of stubbornly trying to figure things out on my own, but even for me there comes a time when the manual, the directions, or the list of frequently asked questions comes in handy.

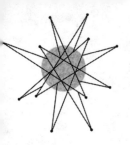

Offline Help

With that little pep talk in mind, take some time to breeze through the Offline Help files (Help ➤ Offline Help ➤ topic of your choosing). The files behave much like Windows 95's Help files, but they give you a lot of how-tos on AOL.

 The Contents tab introduces you to the AOL Help files via the table of contents.

 The Index tab allows you to search an alphabetical listing of the help topics. When you find what you want, double-click the topic.

 The Find tab (Figure A.1) contains a searchable database of topics by related words; this method is probably the easiest offline way for you to find what you want. When you need to find something very specific—such as information on a certain type of sound file—click the Options button on the right to get to some Boolean-like search definers. These will allow you to narrow your search appropriately so you don't have to wade through a mess of entries.

Online Help

Online, you'll have way more resources at your disposal. For one thing, all the Help menu items become active once you've signed on to AOL.

Member Services Online Help

As illustrated in Figure A.2, Member Services Online Help treats you to a well-controlled avalanche of information about the various features of AOL. A must read for the information seeker, you can find out all sorts of little tidbits about the most basic of services

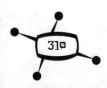

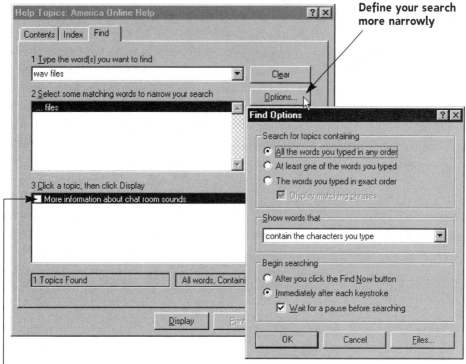

Define your search
more narrowly

More information about WAV files can be found under this Help entry

FIGURE A.1: Searching for offline info about sound files

or go right to the message boards to browse through the answers
to other people's dilemmas. (See *General to Specific Help via Online
Interaction* later in this chapter for tips on message board use.)

Parental Controls

Parental Controls (Figure A.3) allows you to decide what the kids
in your family can do on AOL. Only the master account can access
Parental Controls, so if you've got kids with subaccounts on your
master account, this area is for you. You can decide the age range
appropriate for your child (general, teen, or child) and, through
the Custom Controls button, decide if and how your kid will
experience chat, instant messages, downloading, newsgroups,
e-mail, and the Web.

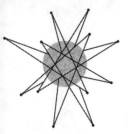

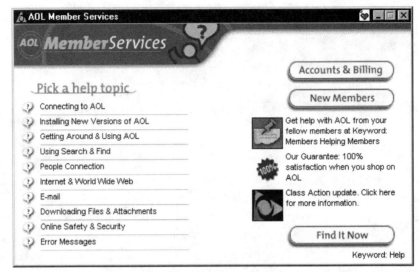

FIGURE A.2: Everything you wanted to know brought to you in the safety of your own home

Control premium surcharged areas
Configure the AOL experience for young kids

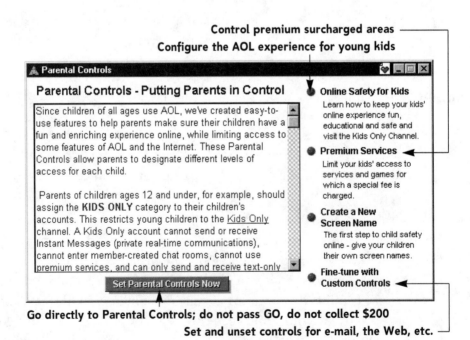

Go directly to Parental Controls; do not pass GO, do not collect $200
Set and unset controls for e-mail, the Web, etc.

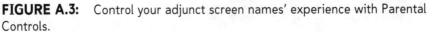

FIGURE A.3: Control your adjunct screen names' experience with Parental Controls.

SECRET

Even if you aren't a parent, you'll want to thoroughly check out Parental Controls; your subaccounts are automatically blocked from these activities: hyperlinks in chat rooms, downloading binary files from newsgroups, and playing premium games. If you wish to prowl with a subaccount, you'll want full access to AOL's features.

HELP WITH KEYWORDS

The Help with Keywords menu item does just that—gives you a few tips on using keywords.

While you're here though, let me define *keyword* for you. A keyword is a word that has been associated with an AOL area; the keyword clearly defines the essence of the area. It is not the same thing as a word used to *search* AOL; a search word could be anything that's touched on in an area. For instance, you can find Heckler's Online through its keyword, **ho**, or you could search for it using the Find button and the search words *irreverent humor*.

TIP

For an exhaustive list of keywords, go to keyword **keyword** (what else?).

ACCOUNTS AND BILLING

At the Accounts and Billing window (Figure A.4), you can perform any convolutions you wish with your personal information—as long as you're signed on as the master account screen name.

313

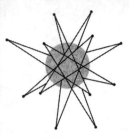

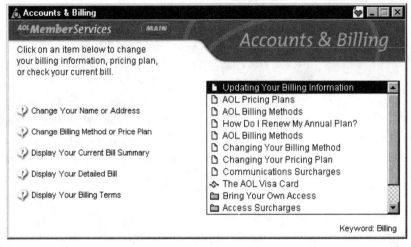

FIGURE A.4: Credit card roulette or close budgeting; everyone has a financial home here at Accounts and Billing.

AOL Access Phone Numbers

At the Accessing America Online screen (Figure A.5), you can play with your access information. Traveling to Taipei? No problem. Switching service providers, but wish to retain your AOL account? A cinch. Wanna buy a snazzy new modem? Don't crowd, ladies and gentlemen, there's room for everyone.

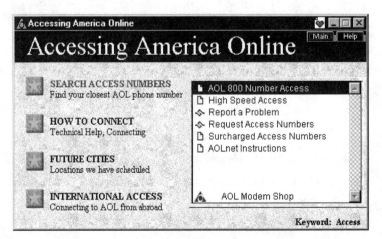

FIGURE A.5: Whatever your little accessing heart desires

What's New in AOL 4.0

Here you can get up to speed on the best, baddest, and bravest of AOL 4's new features. If you just want to get oriented, you can do that too by selecting the Where Is It index and relocating your old favorites.

QuickStart, aka New Member Help

QuickStart: A Guide for New Members (Figure A.6) is super useful for those of us trying to get acclimated to this huge, crazy AOL world. Especially useful, and highly recommended, is Meg's Insider Tips. A little bit sassy, a little bit wise, you can learn something new *and* put a smile on your face by checking this area out.

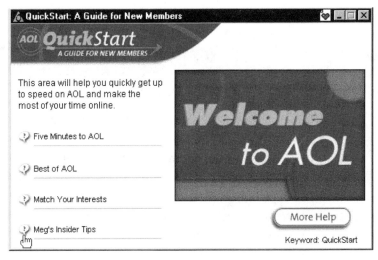

FIGURE A.6:   Quick, no one's looking! Click here and learn something!

Find

Clearly distinguished from the Keyword command (see my explanation under *Help with Keywords*, earlier), the Find button will

search AOL, the Web, AOL's software area, the member database.... See for yourself; Figure A.7 shows your search choices. Bone up on Chapter 6, *Searching with Purpose*, for hints on finding exactly what you want.

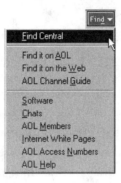

FIGURE A.7: Searching, searching...

General to Specific Help via Online Interaction

Keyword **mhm** is the easiest way to get to the message boards on AOL. These boards are great, let me tell you. The volunteers who answer the questions are knowledgeable and courteous.

Message boards are complex; not only do they have their own rules and etiquette, but there are two kinds, one quite a bit more sophisticated than the other. You won't be surprised to hear that the latter is the new kind, which will gradually replace the old kind.

The Old Type of Message Board

The message board you'll be most familiar with is the old type: white background, fairly limited features (Figure A.8).

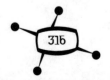

Topics ───────────────── How many posts on each topic ───────────

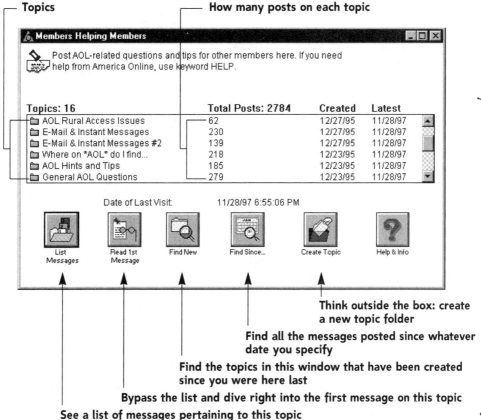

Think outside the box: create
a new topic folder

Find all the messages posted since whatever
date you specify

Find the topics in this window that have been created
since you were here last

Bypass the list and dive right into the first message on this topic

See a list of messages pertaining to this topic

FIGURE A.8: The old type of message board

When you open up a topic to its message list, you'll see something like Figure A.9.

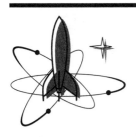

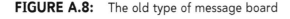

TIP

After you read what the new message boards can do, you'll be wondering how to approximate certain things on the old boards. Signatures are a big one. To include a sig with your posting to the old message board, create it in a text file first, then copy and paste it into your posting.

Read this little blurb to make sure you're in the right place

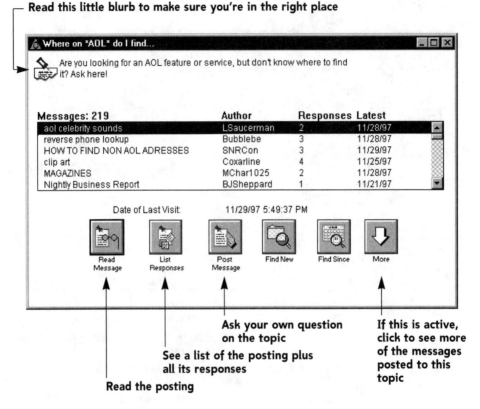

Ask your own question on the topic

See a list of the posting plus all its responses

If this is active, click to see more of the messages posted to this topic

Read the posting

FIGURE A.9: Probing questions answered here

The New Type of Message Board

Elegantly arranged on a succulent bed of pushpins, the new message boards have a lot to offer (Figure A.10).

Let me make just a few comments on the features pointed out in Figure A.10.

The Mark Read button is super useful if you're only looking for specific postings. If some of the message subjects aren't interesting to you, don't waste your time reading them just to make sure you don't have to see them again; instead, use Mark Read to mass-mark everything you've seen so far. You'll never have to see

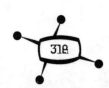

those messages again. (Of course, you can always choose to see past messages by selecting List All or Find Since.)

Make a topic or posting a Favorite Place for easy access

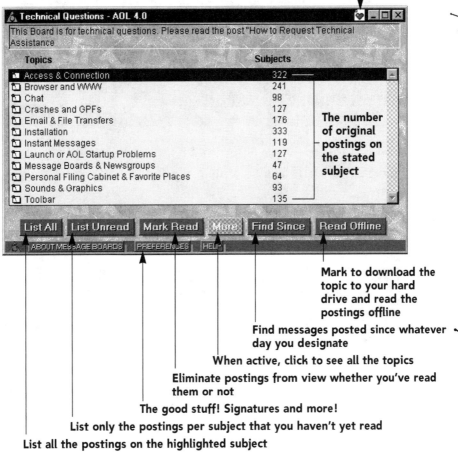

The number of original postings on the stated subject

Mark to download the topic to your hard drive and read the postings offline

Find messages posted since whatever day you designate

When active, click to see all the topics

Eliminate postings from view whether you've read them or not

The good stuff! Signatures and more!

List only the postings per subject that you haven't yet read

List all the postings on the highlighted subject

FIGURE A.10: The new type of message board!

Read Offline isn't just beneficial to those on the limited-access AOL budget; downloaded postings take less time to riffle through and they're easier to archive for future reference. To read a message board topic offline, highlight the topic and click Read Offline. Go to keyword **my boards** to check that the topic

was added successfully. Here you can also choose whether to remove a topic from your Offline reading list—either temporarily or permanently.

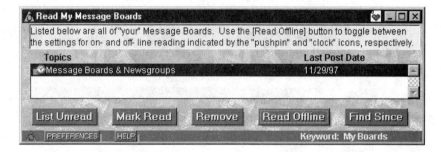

And Preferences! Figure A.11 shows the super-duper customization options available to you on these new message boards.

Tell 'em who you are, invite them to locate/e-mail/IM you

See lists of topics and messages as you please

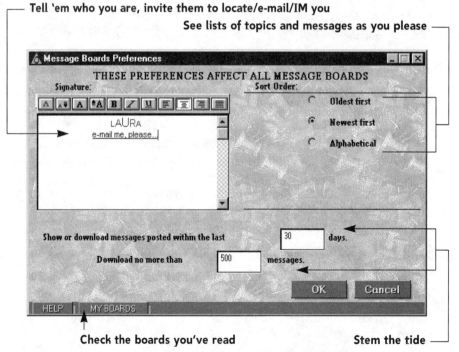

Check the boards you've read

Stem the tide

FIGURE A.11: Alphabetization, interactive signatures, and more!

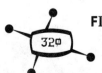

Everything in Figure A.11 is self-explanatory except for the signature feature. You may have noticed—either in Chapters 1 through 3 of this book or on the message boards themselves—that people have done all sorts of wacky things with their signatures, the identifying text that automatically appears at the bottom of each message they post. The most difficult to reproduce without special know-how is the hotlink feature. I explain how to create a hotlink in detail in Chapter 1, but I'll recreate it here for your amusement and edification.

SIGNATURE SECRETS

You can invite other message board readers to e-mail you, locate you, IM you, or view your Web page by including a hotlink in your message board signature. To set this hotlink up:

1. Go to Favorites ➤ Favorite Places and click the New button.

    New

2. In the Add New Folder/Favorite Place box, enter the text you wish to become your hotlink in the top field.

3. In the bottom field, enter the appropriate text from the list below.

HOTLINK TEXT	HOTLINK COMMAND
E-mail me!	mailto:*YourScreenName@aol.com*
IM me!	aol://9293:*YourScreenName*
Locate me!	aol://3548:*YourScreenName*
Check out my Web page!	http://*YourWebPage*
Check out this AOL Area!	aol://1722:*TheKeyword*

Continued

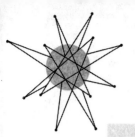

Don't forget to substitute your screen name for *YourScreen-Name*, your URL for *YourWebPage*, and the keyword of your choice for *TheKeyword*.

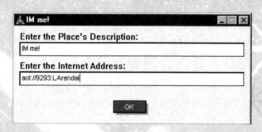

4. Click OK. The new fave place will be added to your Favorite Places entries.

5. Now, to create an automatic signature for your message board postings, click the Preferences button to get into your Message Board Preferences.

6. Drag and drop that hotlinked Fave Place heart over to your Signature box.

Drag'n'drop

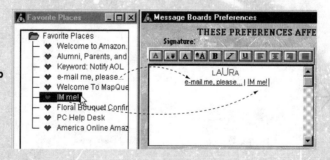

7. If you want to test your signature to make sure it works as planned, create a Signature Tests Only Please message under Members Helping Members. Experiment there.

Back to the message boards themselves: The message listings within a topic also have their own features, shown in Figure A.12.

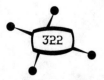

As always, check here to make sure you're within the appropriate topic

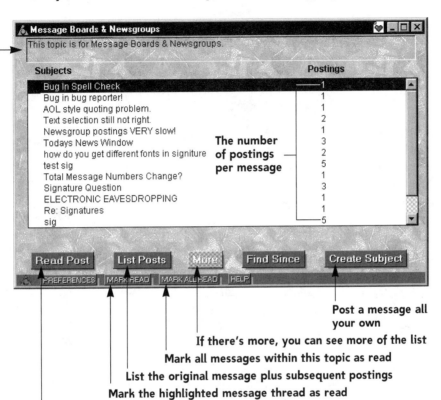

The number of postings per message

Post a message all your own

If there's more, you can see more of the list

Mark all messages within this topic as read

List the original message plus subsequent postings

Mark the highlighted message thread as read

Read the posting(s)

FIGURE A.12: More functions, less hassle

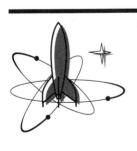

TIP

Checking the number of postings is quite handy if you're looking to browse questions and answers. A message with a posting total of one is a message only; two or more indicate you have a chance of finding a solution to the original question (of course, it's possible that the subsequent messages are confirmations of the original poster's dilemma).

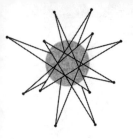

Once you get into a message, you have a few more important options, illustrated in Figure A.13.

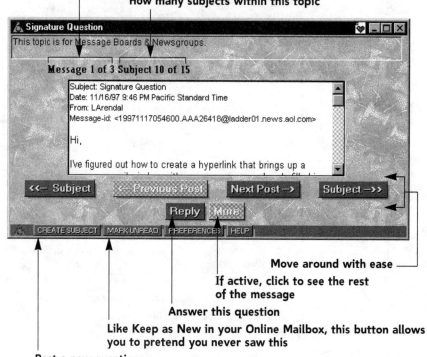

How many messages in this subject thread

How many subjects within this topic

Move around with ease

If active, click to see the rest of the message

Answer this question

Like Keep as New in your Online Mailbox, this button allows you to pretend you never saw this

Post a new question

FIGURE A.13: Ask a question, get an answer.

NOTE

Because the message boards nestled in pushpins are so feature-loaded, it will take a little while for messages you post to actually show up. *A little while* is usually less than 5 minutes.

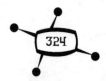

Message Boardiquette

You want your questions answered, right? To earn the respect of the volunteer message board answer elves—and find the solutions to your dilemmas—follow these guidelines:

 Abide by your TOS agreement.

Be nice; no abusive language, no ALL CAPS posts.

As with chat rooms, lurk to get a feel for the tone and topics before posting.

 Read your message over before posting it; make sure that those who want to help you will be able to understand what you're asking.

 Don't post chain letters.

 Don't post advertisements (except on the Classifieds message boards at keyword **classifieds**).

 Refrain from posting messages stating merely "me, too."

 E-mail personal responses directly to the poster of the original message rather than posting such a response.

 Don't post the same message to more than one message board.

Be discreet; don't post personal info about yourself (like your address or phone number).

Read the FAQs to make sure you're following any guidelines specific to that message board.

325

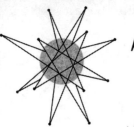

Very Specific Help via Online Interaction

Browsing for tips and flinging questions out to the vast AOL universe is all well and good, but sometimes you need to get more specific. Following are a few ways you can do so.

Area-Specific Help

In every AOL area there is a Help button that will give you advice and information about the area. In addition, you can find support somewhere on AOL for almost any problem you're having. The **Software** area can help you with computer trouble, **Parent Soup** can help relieve child-raising stress, **PF Live** offers financial advice... the list goes on. If you don't know where to turn, click the Find button in the AOL toolbar, choose Find It on AOL, and search for a solution to your troubles.

TIP

Go to keyword **pc help** for some excellent, well-organized help and advice on anything about computers and AOL. There's a Mac section here, too.

Tech Help

When all else fails (but you're not ready to resort to the phone), try Tech Help via e-mail. It's friendly, and it's free.

(?) Ask The Staff   To send a techie staffer a question via e-mail, go to keyword Help and choose a Help topic. In the resultant screen, click the Ask the Staff button on the lower left.

In the More Ways to Get Help window (Figure A.14), you can choose among several options. I've covered the message boards,

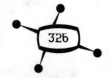

Help Advice and Secrets

where volunteer AOL members answer posted questions, earlier
in this appendix. The next option is to e-mail a technical staff
member your question. Just click the **e-mail** hotlink, choose
from the list of question types (general, technical, Internet, or
billing), type your question into the question field, and click
Send Question (Figure A.15).

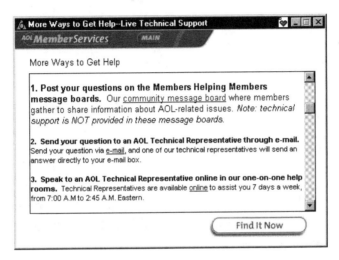

FIGURE A.14: Help! I need somebody!

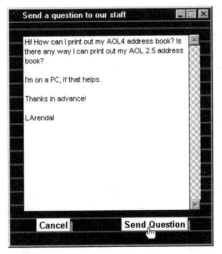

FIGURE A.15: I'm a confused AOL puppy.

To send a suggestion, choose the Make a Suggestion option, then select the AOL area your suggestion pertains to. Type your polite, clearly worded suggestion into the box provided and click Send.

LIVE MEMBERS HELPING MEMBERS HELP

If you don't want to wait for e-mail or your situation is nontechnical but so complicated that you don't feel you can explain it in an e-mail, you can chat with a techie in real time. Open from early in the morning to late into the night, the volunteer-hosted auditorium (which looks just like a chat room) houses patient, supportive Tech Hosts who will gladly help you with your question.

Before you enter the auditorium, keep in mind that usually there are many people in there vying for attention. The Host keeps track of whose turn it is by consulting a list of people who've entered in order of appearance; your mission—should you choose to accept—is to lurk quietly until the Host calls on you directly and invites you to ask your question.

To enter the Tech Live auditorium, go to keyword **Help** and choose a Help topic, click the Ask the Staff button on the lower left, and, in the More Ways to Get Help window (Figure A.14), choose the **online** hotlink. At the Technical Representatives dialog box, check that you're connecting within the time specified in the More Ways to Get Help list, and click the Go There button.

TOS HELP

If you feel someone is violating their Terms of Service agreement and it's interfering with your inalienable right to have a good time on AOL, go to keyword **TOS** and follow the appropriate steps to report them. There are many types of TOS violations, the steps to follow are clear, and I've covered most of them in Chapters 2 and 3, so I won't repeat myself needlessly here. Suffice it to say, AOL officials are very concerned with ensuring that

AOL is a safe and enjoyable place for all to gather, and your concerns will be taken seriously.

VERY SPECIFIC HELP BY PHONE

You can't connect, and you're desperate! The following list will help you connect to a live knowledge-riddled human:

Technical questions for Windows users	1-888-265-8006
Technical questions for Mac users	1-888-265-8007
Screen name and/or password difficulties	1-888-265-8004
To get AOL access numbers	1-888-265-8005
Tech support within the US and Canada	1-800-827-3338
Sales and billing questions	1-888-265-8003
Account credit requests (for instance, if an AOL error forced you to stay longer in a premium area than you intended)	1-888-265-8009
TTY for the hearing impaired	1-800-759-3323
Product information	1-888-265-8001
Orders	1-888-265-8002
Cancellation requests	1-888-265-8008
International callers	1-703-264-1184
France: member services	01-69-19-94-50
Germany: member services	0-180-531-3164
UK: member services	0-800-376-5432

If you don't find the number you need in this list, go to keyword **callaol** to find the telephone number you need.

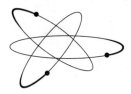

INDEX

Note to the Reader: First level entries are in **bold**. Page numbers in **bold** indicate the principal discussion of a topic or the definition of a term. Page numbers in *italic* indicate illustrations.

NUMBERS AND SYMBOLS

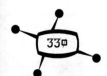

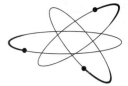

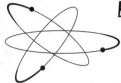

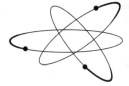

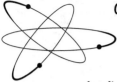

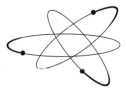

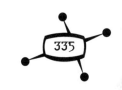

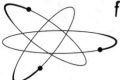

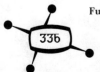

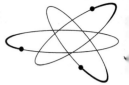

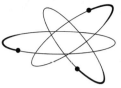

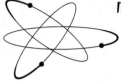

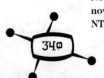

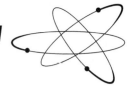

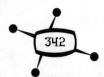

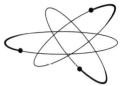

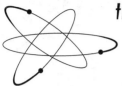

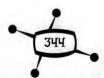

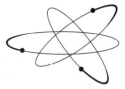

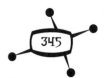

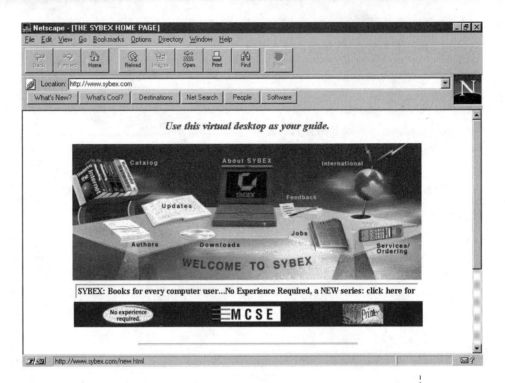